DEPED PORTAL UTILIZATION OF PUBLIC ELEMENTARY TEACHERS AND ACADEMIC PERFORMANCE OF LEARNERS

by

CRISTINA BAGAPORO TAAY LPT, MaEd

ISBN:

Hardbound-978-621-495-173-4

Softbound/Paperback-978-621-495-174-1

MOBI/KINDLE-978-621-495-175-8

Published by:

Poetry Planet Book Publishing House

Rosario, Pozorrubio, Pangasinan, Philippines

Contact Number:075-615-5455

Email: maritesritumalta@gmail.com

DEDICATION

This published research work is dedicated with love and gratitude to my family;

my husband, **Reynold C. Taay,**

for his never ending love;

to my children,

Janela Cassandra, Gabriel Kristoffer, **Jairos Kristan** and **Rhinoa Katrina**,

for being my inspiration to live, to dream and to strive,

my parents,

Benigno (+) and **Elena** (+)

To all my friends who encouraged and supported me,

To my ever-supportive Principal at Silanganan Elementary School,

Dr. Marilyn M. Laureno,

for giving me the opportunity to be part of SES,

To all my colleagues,

They are always willing to lend a helping hand.

To my strong pillar, my source of wisdom and knowledge

the **LORD JESUS CHRIST,**

who made this humble success possible.

I thank you all!

CBT

ABSTRACT

DEPED PORTAL UTILIZATION OF PUBLIC ELEMENTARY TEACHERS AND ACADEMIC PERFORMANCE OF LEARNER

Public elementary teachers have access to a variety of tools and resources through the Department of Education (DepEd) Portal, a digital platform that supports teaching and learning in the classroom. The portal provides curriculum-aligned resources that aim to improve the standard of instruction in public elementary schools, such as lesson plans, teaching aids, and assessment tools.

This study focused on examining the connection between students' academic achievement and how public elementary teachers use the DepEd Portal. Through this study, the researcher hope to pinpoint the elements that affect how the portal is used and how that usage affects students' academic achievement.

Using descriptive correlational research design and distributed questionnaires for 150 respondents, the study found that: The level of utilization of Public Elementary Teachers of DEPED portal as asses by Master Teachers, Grade Level Chairman, and themselves as to Student Learning Materials, Teacher's Teaching Guide, and Video Lessons are highly utilized by the respondents; There is a significant difference in the assessment of the respondents in the level of utilization of DEPED portal. This further indicates that there is a significant difference in the assessment of the two groups of respondents or the assessment of the three groups are all different; The Academic performance of Grade 5 learners increased from 1st to 2nd Quarter based on General Weighted Average (GWA); DEPED portal utilization in terms of video lessons and the academic performance of the learners during the two quarters. This further indicates that if the teachers highly utilized the video lessons in the DEPED portal, the academic performance of the learners will get better and vice versa. Cannot access the portal because no accounts yet due to difficulty in creating one, Registration process is time-consuming, and School does not have a stable connection are few of the challenges encountered by the respondents. They highly recommend that the school head assigned teachers who will maintain the school portal and monitors their performance religiously and ensure that all personnel assigned in

LRMDS will be updated on the floor of confirmation of accounts to avoid delays.

On the account of conclusions presented in this study, the following recommendations are drawn: Conduct a training program for public Elementary teachers on how to effectively use the DepEd Portal. Ensure that the DepEd Portal is updated regularly with relevant and accurate information that can support the teaching and learning process. This can include lesson plans, assessment tools, and other resources that are aligned with the curriculum; Monitor the utilization of the DepEd Portal by public elementary teachers and track the academic performance of learners. This can help determine if there is a correlation between the two variables and if the portal is contributing to improved learning outcomes; establish a feedback mechanism to gather insights from public elementary teachers and learners on their experiences in using the DepEd Portal. This can help identify areas for improvement and inform future initiatives to support teaching and learning in public elementary schools; and Collaborate with other stakeholders, such as parents and community members, to promote the utilization of the DepEd Portal and support the academic performance of learners. This can include information campaigns and other initiatives.

TABLE OF CONTENTS

Chapter 1

THE PROBLEM AND ITS BACKGROUND

This chapter presents the background of the study, statement of the problem, hypothesis, scope and delimitation and the significance of the study.

Introduction

The DepEd portal is designed to give access to high-quality learning and teaching materials like Learning Material, Lesson Plans, Learning Guides, Learning Modules, and Full Courses that are aligned with the K–12 curriculum. These can be utilized as the foundation for teaching and learning or as a supplement. It serves as a clearinghouse for information. Further, through DepEd portal, LRMDS is created. It is a system for providing accessible teaching and learning materials (TLMs) and resources for professional development, as specified in DM 82, s.2017. It contains rules, criteria, and specifications for assessing, evaluating, harvesting, modifying, developing, and producing high-quality contextualized, localized, and indigenous resources. Through the LR Portal, it is an online repository or library for downloadable TLMs that are presented in terms of relevance and suitability to the curriculum.

In response to educational needs, the LR Portal allows users to access digitized versions of some contextualized and localized TLMs. LRMDS also enables for the posting of learning resource content (DO 35, s.2010). It unquestionably has a lot of promising potentials for the end users, namely are teachers. Its accessibility, on the other hand, would always equate to its efficacy. The majority of teachers complain about the amount of time it takes to access the portal. Each attempt to gain access could not even guarantee a 100 percent success rate. Many people may have overlooked the practical use of the site and the other tools that instructors use in its absence, so it's unclear how well it was working.

Teachers should generally seek for and design learning materials that meet the quality and consistency standards indicated below. According to the DepEd LRMDS manual, professionally developed learning materials should take into account the following: clearly and concisely articulated learning goals and objectives; appropriately considered the student grade level and reading level; content should be engaging, relevant, and up-to-date to the learning competencies; appropriate to use in differentiated learning opportunities; content should be well-designed and appealing to students; and the general concept should be adaptable for individual learning styles and learning needs. In this regard, the researcher conducts a study that will dig-in the influence that utilization of teachers of DepEd Portal in enhancing the academic performance of students and eventually recommends for the improvement of the said portal for the welfare of teachers, learners, and the school.

Background of the Study

The complex ecology for controlling teaching and learning practices was clearly characterized by the dynamics of learning. With so many learning and teaching resources available online, it is easy to ignore the Department of Education's cyber backyard for educators, the Learning Resources Management and Development System (LRMDS).

Eventually, LRMDS is a system for providing accessible teaching and learning materials (TLMs) and resources for professional development, as specified in DM 82, s.2017. It contains rules, criteria, and specifications for assessing, evaluating, harvesting, modifying, developing, and producing high-quality contextualized, localized, and indigenous resources. Through the LR portal, it is an online repository or library for downloadable TLMs that are framed in relevance and suitability to the curriculum.

The researcher identified some problems like absence of a clearer format as to the guidelines in producing learning resources, time constraint when accessing the portal, lack of instructions and trainings, lack of motivation for the teachers to produce an LR, lack of monitoring, system glitch like not being able to access to the downloadable files, and no internet connection that serves as the very backbone in getting into the portal itself. So, when all else fails, teachers use all means available to them to gain access to the resources they require from other beneficial sites or sources. Thus, knowing how important the portal, the school administrators seek for the solution of the problems by asking support from the school stakeholders ensuring the utilization of LRMDS by the teachers for the welfare of their learners. The proponent of the study believe that Learning Resources increase its applicability especially on today's situation to strengthen the learning continuity project of the Department of Education.

In Silanganan Elementary School, where the researcher is presently assigned as ICT Coordinator, she instructed teachers to utilize the LRMDS portal of the school in harvesting instructional materials to be used in their teaching. She also encourages teachers to create instructional materials and upload it to the portal by recognizing them by giving certificates of recognition which can be used in their promotion. Hence, the real essence is not only to recognized their skills and effort but also to make sure that there are available LR in the portal.

To determine and eventually prove the impact of DepEd portal utilization of teachers in their pupils' academic performance, the researcher decided to conduct the study entitled, "DepEd Portal Utilization of Public Elementary Teachers and Academic Performance of Learners." She believes that through this research, questions about the premise will therefore be answered.

Statement of the Problem

This study aimed to determine the level of DepEd portal utilization of public elementary teachers and academic performance of learners.

Specifically, this study answered the following questions:

1. What is the level of utilization of Public Elementary Teachers of DepEd portal as asses by Grade Level Chairman and teachers as to:

1.1 Student Learning Materials;

1.2 Teacher's Teaching Guides and

1.3 Video Lessons?

2. Is there a significant difference on the assessment of the two groups of respondents on the level of utilization of DepEd Portal when the aforementioned variables are considered?

3. What is the Academic performance of Grade 5 learners for the 1st and 2nd Quarter based on General Weighted Average (GWA)?

4. Is there a significant relationship between the level of DepEd portal utilization and the academic performance of learners?

5. What are the challenges encountered and solutions offered in the utilization of DepEd Portal?

6. Based on the findings of the study, what training plan may be proposed?

Hypotheses

H_o 1: There is no significant difference on the assessment of the two groups of respondents on the level of utilization of DepEd Portal.

H_o 2: There is no significant relationship between the level of DepEd portal utilization and the academic performance of learners.

Scope and Delimitation of the Study

This study focused on determining the level of DepEd Portal utilization of public elementary teachers and academic performance of learners in selected public elementary schools in North II District, Division of Caloocan during the School Year 2022-2023.

Further, it utilized one hundred 150 teachers in North II District Schools specifically Sto. Nino Elementary School, Bagong Silang Elementary School, Gabriela Silang Elementary School, Rene Cayetano Elementary School, and Silanganan Elementary School. The study investigated the following: The level of utilization of Public Elementary Teachers of DepEd portal as to Student Learning Materials, Teacher's Teaching Guide, and video lessons; The significant difference on the level of utilization of DepEd Portal of Teacher- respondents; The Academic performance of Grade V learners for the 1st and 2nd Quarter based on GWA; and The significant relationship between the level of DepEd portal utilization and the academic performance of learners.

Significance of the Study

The outcomes of this study can significantly contributed in realizing the effectiveness of DepEd portal utilization of public elementary teachers in the academic performance of learners in selected public elementary schools. This study may be deemed beneficial to the following:

Learners. They can profit a lot of from the study since revelation of this research will help them to sustain in studying through the utilization of DepEd Portal.

Teachers. The findings of the study will deliver awareness to them on how DepEd portal influences their learners learning accumulation through the utilization of their teacher of the portal and might design a student learning program through DepEd Portal.

Grade Level Chairperson. The findings of the study will enlighten them the real scenario on the effect of DepEd portal and eventually might design a grade level-based program that will address the challenges in using the said portal.

Master Teachers. The study will eventually make them realize the benefits of LRMDS and will give credit to the teachers who will create LRs and utilize available LRs in the portal as one way of intensifying the use of LRMDS portal and enjoy the very reason why the Department of Education mandated the creation and utilization of the said portal.

School Heads. The results of this study would serve as bases for a strategic planning on sustaining and improving the school-based Portal intended for teachers and pupils to increase learners' mastery.

Parents. The study will make them realize that there are other avenues in gathering learning instructional materials that they can use in giving follow-up learning to their child.

Researcher. The conduct of the study will enhance her skills and competencies in finding out solutions in every challenge she encounters in her profession through research.

Future Researchers. This analysis is going to be a helpful reference for the researchers who would really like to analyze similar topic. What is more, the results of the study may offer knowledge or data about the influences of DepEd Portal in the academic performance of the learners.

Chapter 2

REVIEW OF RELATED LITERATURE AND STUDIES

This part of research presents an outline of related literature and studies which are reviewed by the researcher with the concepts that would facilitate in responding specific issues of this study.

Technology and the LRMDS Portal

Technology allows individuals connect and even work online without the need for face-to-face interaction in times of disaster, providing inventive and resilient solutions to counteract disruption. As firms adopt new technologies for communicating and working, this results in a slew of system adjustments (Mark and Semaan, as cited in Dayagbil et al., 2021). However, technological obstacles such as internet access, particularly in areas where there are no signals, can be the most significant impediment to teaching and learning continuity, particularly for academic institutions that have chosen online learning as a teaching mode.

Ninety percent of the world's student population has been harmed by the nationwide shutdown of educational institutions in an attempt to restrict the virus's spread (UNESCO, 2020). The goal of this research is to look into the issues of maintaining teaching and learning continuity during the epidemic. From the standpoint of learners, it is critical to explore how to lessen the immediate impact of school closures on learning continuity. Furthermore, because teachers are the ones who provide and support the learning process, their viewpoints are just as significant as the learners'. Teachers should effectively address the present issues of facilitating learner learning, learner differentiation, and learner-centeredness, as well as being prepared to serve as facilitators on remote learning platforms (Chi-Kin Lee, 2020; Edizon, 2020; Hijazi, 2020).

In the study conducted by Torbila (2021) she claimed that learning resources have not been developed, stored, or shared as quickly or easily as they have been in the digital era. The impact of teacher factors on their use of the Department of Education's Learning Resource Management and Development System was investigated in this descriptive-correlational study. The 1030 teacher-respondents from the DepEd Biliran Division were selected using a simple random selection technique. The data was collected via a survey questionnaire and analyzed using descriptive statistics, Pearson r, and multiple regression analysis. The majority of responders used the LRMDS portal fairly, according to the results. Their age, sex, and civil status have a negative significant impact on their LRMDS utilization, whereas their highest educational attainment and years in teaching have a favorable significant impact. The use of LRMDS is thought to be linked to the teachers' professional development and tried – and - true experiences. A recommendation is given about constant teacher empowerment in the development and digital dissemination of learning resources via the DepEd portal.

Since the Department of Education has taken advantage of this platform, learning through engagement has become the new normal. The Learning Resources Management and Development System (LRMDS) is one such effort that was built with the help of the STRIVE (Strengthening Implementation of Visayas Education) is a program run by the Australian government. Southern Leyte, Tacloban City, Maasin City, and Baybay City have nearly 100% participation rate in the LRMDS portal registration in Region VIII (Learning Resource Portal/Dashboard, Admin Panel, RO8 s. 2018).

Furthermore, Susara (2016), on the other hand, discovered issues with the DepEd LR portal, such as the lack of a clear format for learning resources, delays in accessing the portal, a lack of knowledge about how to use the portal, unmotivated teachers in producing learning resources, system glitches, and poor internet access. As a result, the researcher determined that it was necessary to investigate the teachers' profiles as well as their use of LRMDS to see if the former has an impact on the latter. The Department of Education's Learning Resource Management and Development System is a platform that, when fully utilized, has the ability to significantly improve the quality of education that public school instructors provide to their students. Teachers, on the other hand, are at the forefront of this strategy for managing digital learning resources. It is critical that they have the information and skills necessary to create, store, and share high-quality learning resources, either through additional studies or through their extensive teaching experience. If the LRMDS is to be evaluated, the willingness of the teachers to use everything it has to offer is critical (Torbila, 2021).

Thus, teachers were less eager, if not unwilling, to contribute their own learning materials for review, quality assurance, and sharing through the DepEd learning portals or other similar online platforms, according to Sipahi (2020). This could be due to a lack of sufficient TLM options being available (Mapunda, as cited in Torbila, 2021).

According to Llego (2022) the Department of Education (DepEd) is in a difficult predicament as it is forced to move out of its comfort zone, from traditional face-to-face classroom instruction to discovering innovative and unusual ways to ensure education continuity in the face of the COVID-19 pandemic. The DepEd Commons—an online platform to promote the ongoing delivery of basic education to Filipino learners—is one of the strategies the Department is working on to improve the distance learning delivery modality in response to the health crisis. Initially conceived as a "reaction" to the 2012 Paris Open Education Resources (OER) Declaration to encourage the collection and distribution of free online instructional supplementary materials, it is swiftly expanding into a gateway that will accommodate numerous learning delivery modes.

Due of the current Covid19 pandemic, traditional or face-to-face schooling is discouraged in order to limit disease spread. The Department of Education Malaybalay City Division, like all other local divisions, has responded to this demand by developing learning modules as an alternate learning mode. This new normal in education is difficult for both teachers, who serve as facilitators of learning, and students, who will receive lessons in this new method. The major problem is determining how to make learning materials or modules effective in terms of learners' knowledge acquisition and application despite the lack of face-to-face interaction between teacher and student (Abendaño, 2020).

According to DepEd Tambayan (2021) the LRMDS is a web-based catalogue and online library of resources for learning, teaching, and professional development. It consists of four (4) integrated sub-systems: (i) assessment and evaluation; (ii) development, acquisition, and production; (iii) storage and maintenance; and (iv) publication and delivery, all of which are intended to support increased distribution and access to learning, teaching, and professional-development resources at the regional, division, and school levels.

Moreover, in the Negros Oriental Learning Resource Portal (2021), it is reported that the LRMDS is a web-based catalogue and repository of learning, teaching and professional development resources. It functions as a clearinghouse. That is, the LRMDS provides information about the location of resources (hardcopy and softcopy) and allows users of the system to access directly digitized versions of resources that are published and stored within the LRMDS repository. It is also a quality assurance system providing support to DepEd Regions, Divisions and Schools in the selection and acquisition of quality digital and non-digital resources in response to identified local educational needs.

Performance evaluation techniques are used to assess how well policies, plans, and other activities are being implemented. In education, introduced programs' success is evaluated in a similar manner. For instance, Man (2019) suggested an indicator system for gauging academic success from the standpoint of quality management. This idea is in line with Castillo's (2019) findings, which suggest that educational institutions should be assessed using data on I the outputs intended to be produced, (ii) the inputs required to produce the outputs, (iii) quantitative measurements of each input and output, and (iv) the technical relationship between inputs and outputs. Determining the effectiveness score, which is the difference between actual and anticipated graduation rates, is another way for evaluating educational efficiency that has been proposed in recent literature. By analyzing the measuring characteristics of effectiveness scores produced from regression residuals, Horn et al. (2019) demonstrated the method's validity. A learner's core competencies indicator system was also established by Srisakda et al. (2017). This type of indication system evaluates pupils' abilities to communicate, think critically, solve problems, apply life skills, and use technology.\

Wao (2017) stated that indicator systems hide gaps in educational quality, despite the fact that they have been effective in specific situations. Despite the fact that the study was limited to the basic educational system in Malaysia, the paper demonstrated that basic education indicators do not necessarily convert into exceptional performance on international assessments like the Trends in International Mathematics and Science Study (TIMSS). Therefore, utilizing different strategies may be advantageous in various applications. The use of tools for descriptive analysis is another strategy that has been employed in recent literature. For instance, Junio-Sabio et al. (2020) employed a descriptive examination of the typical grade level learning outcomes of elementary pupils in the Philippines to make this determination. For evaluating students' academic achievement, skills/abilities exams are frequently used in the basic education literature in addition to indicator systems, descriptive analysis, and inferential techniques. For instance, Bietenbeck et al (2019) assessment of basic education students in East Africa's literacy and numeracy skills. The literacy test evaluated four skills in the following sequence of increasing difficulty: (1) letter recognition, (2) word recognition, (3) paragraph reading, and (4) short story reading. Similar to this, the numeracy test evaluated six skills: counting, number recognition, rank ordering, addition, subtraction, and multiplication. Tseng et al. (2018) created a standardized reading-literacy sample test for seventh-grade English (L2) students and gathered student work and comments from participating teachers and students. Students had to look for lost dogs as part of the scenario-based reading assignment (Tseng et al., 2018).

VESPARCH, an online group examination of verbal and spatial thinking, was created as a result of a study by Badger and Mellanby (2018) to assess basic ability (or fluid intelligence) in students enrolled in basic education in the UK. According to the study's findings, it is possible to identify students who are underachieving academically in comparison to their potential by comparing their VESPARCH scores with school attainment metrics.

The Implementation of LRMDS Portal

Teachers create LR/TR/PDM at the school or cluster level for use in the classroom and regional training. As part of the AIP/SIP process, these resources are typically generated in response to LR planning. These materials might be updated for the LRMDS repository or added to the LRMDS catalogue. Schools should follow these Guidelines and Processes when creating locally tailored LR/TR/PDM materials to guarantee that educational and technical standards are met. All teacher-created resources that are meant to be cataloged in LRMDS and, if digital, uploaded to the LRMDS repository, must first go through assessment and evaluation by the School before moving on to the Division to Region (DepEd Naga, 2019). Thus, The Region shall categorize, replicate, and/or reconstruct any digital materials identified and approved for inclusion in the LRMDS by the Regional LRMDS QA team. The Division LRMDS QA Team tests and evaluates non-digital teacher-developed materials before the Division can replicate them and catalog them in the LRMDS. The Division and Region should be aware of the LR/TR/PDMs being generated locally through the DEPD/REDP planning process and should actively solicit submissions of locally produced materials from schools.

Unless a comment is extremely vague, evaluators should add the evaluation criteria number from the checklist that corresponds to the comment or comments it relates to. The page, screen, or location of the issue being raised within the resource must also be specified. If at all feasible, please provide a Xerox or screen grab of the problem. This will help to address any flaws in the resource's accuracy, consistency, or usability. Materials that do not pass the evaluation because of minor factual or editorial flaws may be suggested for improvement. The Region LRMDS Development and Production Team typically redevelops DepED-owned materials (DepEd Region V, 2019).

Challenges in Utilizing LRMDS Portal

The LRMDS serves as a clearinghouse for the following purposes: Giving users of the system access to and downloading directly digitized versions of resources that are published and stored in multiple formats within the LRMDS repository; and Serving as a Web-based portal with a searchable catalogue and online repository of learning, teaching, and professional development resources. According to the framework for LRMDS, it intends to give teachers and students in both elementary and secondary schools a technological foundation for evaluating, acquiring, modifying, producing, and disseminating high-quality learning and teaching resources. It requires a committee made up of the school librarian, the LRMDS coordinator, and the coordinator for information and communication technology (ICT). In the DepEd Order 76, series of 2011, recognizing its potential, DepEd urges the adoption and implementation of LRMDS across the country (Susara, 2016).

In the study conducted by Susara (2016), she reiterated that for small schools like Lindawan National High School and Baguio City National High School-Hillside Annex, time is what they don't have to focus on LRMDS. "8 lang kami dito tapos 8 subjects. Kung titignan mo, hindi kami gaanong maka-focus sa paggawa ng ganyan. Honestly, mahirap magkaroon ng time para gawin," Mary Jane Reyes, Baguio City National High School-Hillside Annex LRMDS Coordinator, admitted. The same sentiment was expressed by Mildred Gayaden, Lindawan National High School LRMDS Coordinator. "Sa school setting namin, pipito lang kami. Sa small school, madaming appended duties na iba so siyempre, hindi namin maasikaso lahat. Kulang kami ng time para doon (LRMDS). Siyempre mas priority namin ang teaching kaya wala masyadong time para gumawa ng resources na isa-submit sa Division Office (DO)," she narrated.

An operational Internet connection is the most critical component for using the LRMDS portal. Every school has access to the Internet. However, the vast majority of them lack a reliable connection. And that is only the start.

The first thing that must do after the Internet is stable is to complete the lengthy registration process. The registration process for the coordinators takes days or perhaps months. The LRMDS Coordinator should have access to the site since they would be in charge of overseeing the implementation of LRMDS, right? Marianne Gorinto, the LRMDS coordinator for Baguio City National High School-Fort del Pilar, and Maricris Clavio, the coordinator for San Vicente National High School, are unable to use the portal because they do not even have accounts yet.

First, there is a difficulty in signing-in. "Ang hirap mag-log-in," LRMDS Coordinator of Magsaysay NHS Lorraine Gabay said. Additionally, Baguio City NHS Hillside-Annex Reyes also experienced the same thing and contacted the DO. "Kahapon nga, galing ako dun (DO), nagtanong ako kung bakit hindi ko mabuksan 'yung account ko dun. Sabi na medyo yata nagkaproblema kaya hindi pa ako makapasok sa network ng LRMDS," she explained. Marjorie Saingan, Sto.Tomas NHS LRMDS Coordinator, finished the first step but no luck in accessing uploaded LRs. "I can access the portal because I'm already registered, however, I cannot look into the download portal," she said. Hence, registering to the portal is time-consuming; signing-in, a hassle; and accessing the download portal, a difficulty.

An operational Internet connection is the most critical component for using the LRMDS portal. Every school has access to the Internet. However, the vast majority of them lack a reliable connection. And that is only the start. The first thing that must do after the Internet is stable is to complete the lengthy registration process. The registration process for the coordinators takes days or perhaps months.

The LRMDS Coordinator should have access to the site since they would be in charge of overseeing the implementation of LRMDS, right?

Marianne Gorinto, the LRMDS coordinator for Baguio City National High School-Fort del Pilar, and Maricris Clavio, the coordinator for San Vicente National High School, are unable to use the portal because they do not even have accounts yet. It demonstrates that poor or even nonexistent communication is the main issue with LRMDS. To carry out the program's aims and visions, the LRMDS coordinators and LRMDS DO should collaborate. The system, in Yamson's words, "is a collective project."

It is neither the fault of the teachers nor the DO that there aren't any seminars, workshops, or other such events aimed at spreading LRMDS. Everything comes down to a money shortage. LRMDS is a development that DepEd is acknowledging. The lack of financing, however, indicates the contrary.

Benefits of Utilizing DepEd Portals

One of the problems during the epidemic is the kind of educational materials that schools would use, regardless of the sort of instruction. To support their teaching and students' needs, educators look for learning materials wherever they can. Additionally, the division provided access to so many e-learning materials for teachers that they occasionally were perplexed by the selection. As a result, during the academic year 2020–2021, observations, reflections, and experiences led to the idea of a one-stop shop for learning resources. Examples include giving teachers multiple links to all learning resources for self-learning modules, radio and video lessons, and activity sheets for bridging activities, among others. Various focal points and process owners managing the resources resulted in the development of multiple connections.

One of the problems during the epidemic is the kind of educational materials that schools would use, regardless of the sort of instruction. To support their teaching and students' needs, educators look for learning materials wherever they can. Additionally, the division provided access to so many e-learning materials for teachers that they occasionally were perplexed by the selection. As a result, during the academic year 2020–2021, observations, reflections, and experiences led to the idea of a one-stop shop for learning resources. Examples include giving teachers multiple links to all learning resources for self-learning modules, radio and video lessons, and activity sheets for bridging activities, among others.

Effective educational resources make positive connections with learners' knowledge, experience, and identity. Learning is an active process that involves many different kinds of connections. People learn best when they are able to connect new learning with what they already know and can do.Various focal points and process owners managing the resources resulted in the development of multiple connections. The following are the portal's distinguishing features: (1) well-structured self-learning modules for Kindergarten through Grade 12, electronic books used in our bichronous classes, and supplemental learning resources like radio lessons, video lessons, and admirable research results for reference; (2) contextualized learning materials created and produced by innovators in educational resources; (3) current, popular, and highly relevant types of educational content. As the Google site is free and very simple to use with a user-friendly layout, it also contains a personalized tutorial on how to use the K-12 ebooks, (6) no expense in constructing the portal, and (7) contact information in case of any issues regarding the portal's use (Beveridge, 2019).

Synthesis of the Reviewed Studies

The study focused on how teachers might use the DepEd Portal to improve students' academic achievement. The investigation has also attested to the fact that learning dynamics clearly define the complicated system for managing teaching and learning practices. Just like other literature and researches featured in this study, this research is an overlook on thc Learning Resources Management and Development System that pertains to the Department of Education's online playground for educators, given the abundance of learning and teaching resources available online (LRMDS).

The researcher makes sure that the LRMDS concept—described in DM 82, s. 2017 as a system for delivering accessible teaching and learning materials (TLMs) and resources for professional development—is upheld. It includes guidelines, standards, and requirements for identifying, classifying, selecting, developing, changing, and manufacturing high-quality contextualized, localized, and indigenous materials. It is an online library or repository accessible through the LR portal that houses TLMs that can be downloaded and is organized according to how well they relate to the curriculum. It provides a technical basis for assessing, acquiring, adapting, developing, producing and distributing quality learning and teaching resource materials for students and instructional support materials for teachers. It also provides access to quality resources from the Regions, Divisions, School level: including information on quantity and quality and location of textbooks and supplementary materials, and cultural expertise, access to learning, teaching and professional development resources in digital format and locates resources in print format and hard copy.

Additionally, it reaffirmed that users of the LR Portal may access digital copies of some contextualized and localized TLMs. Additionally, LRMDS permits the publishing of content for learning resources. For the end users, who are teachers, it undoubtedly offers a lot of exciting potentials. On the other hand, its usability would always correlate to its effectiveness. Most educators express frustration with the length of time it takes to access the portal. On the contrary, the present study deals primarily on the utilization of teachers of DEPED portal and how this move influences the academic performance of their learners while the mentioned literature and study mostly tackled the challenges that the teachers, students, and even other school personnel experiences before, during and after they use the said portal.

Overall, the linked literature and studies reviewed by the study's proponent have supplied useful insights and recommendations on how the current research should go or be conducted. Related studies, in particular, benefited the researcher in the formulation of the current research's concept.

Theoretical Framework

The TPACK theory, developed by Punya Mishra and Matthew J. Koehler (as cited in Kartal et al., 2016) focusing on technological knowledge (TK), pedagogical knowledge (PK), and content knowledge (CK), provides a productive approach to many of the dilemmas that teachers face when implementing educational technology (edtech) in their classrooms. The Technological, Pedagogical, and Content Knowledge (TPACK) framework outlines how content (what is being taught) and pedagogy (how the teacher imparts that content) must form the foundation for any effective edtech integration by distinguishing between these three types of knowledge. This is important because, in order to improve students' learning experiences, the technology being implemented must communicate the content and support the pedagogy.

TPACK is a technology integration framework that identifies three types of knowledge instructors need to combine for successful Edtech integration—technological, pedagogical, and content knowledge. Technological Pedagogical Content Knowledge (TPACK) is the effectiveness of the delivery of the lesson with technology integration. It is an ideal application in all aspects of learning, which are all important in the teaching and learning process. TPACK is an essential part of the education system today as it incorporates the growing demand on the use of technology in the classroom as well as continuing the focus on the content and how we teach it. Therefore, it sets up education for the future as well as setting up the students for their future.

Relevant technical resources (hardware, software, apps, related knowledge literacy activities, and so on) are best used to teach and direct students toward a stronger, more rigorous understanding of the subject matter, according to the TPACK system. Within the TPACK system, the three forms of information – TK, PK, and CK – are thus merged and recombined in different ways. Technological pedagogical knowledge (TPK) describes the relationships and interactions between technological tools and specific pedagogical practices, while pedagogical content knowledge (PCK) describes the same between pedagogical practices and specific learning objectives, and technological content knowledge (TCK) describes the same between technologies and learning objectives. These three fields are then combined to form TPACK which consider the connections between them all and recognizes that educators are working in a dynamic environment.

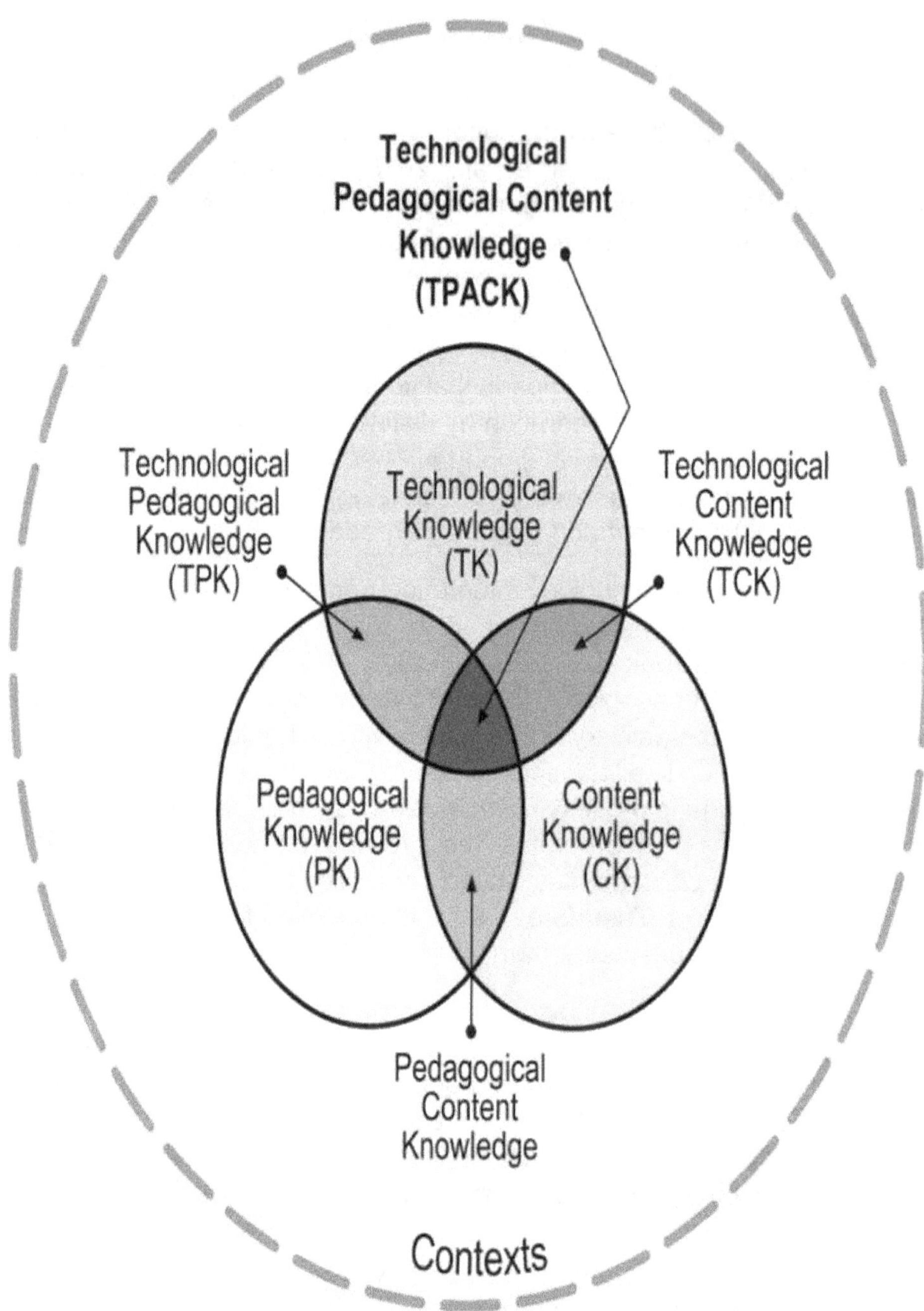

Figure 1: Punya Mishra and Matthew J. Koehler's Framework
2017 TPACK

Conceptual Framework

Every figure in the conceptual framework illustrates the study's conceptualization on the Level of Utilization of Public Elementary Teachers of DEPED Portal: this area of the present study deals with the gathering of data form Student Learning Materials, Teacher's Teaching Guide, and video lessons The researcher believes that by determining the level of utilization of DepEd Portal, she will be able to establish a solid foundation for determining the study's credibility; The Academic performance of Grade V learners for the 1st and 2nd Quarter: The researcher's goal in this study is to determine the influence of DepEd Portal on the academic performance of learners; Sustainability Plan. The researcher believes that through this, she will eventually create a sustainability plan for the utilization of DepEd Portal of the elementary teachers to enhance the academic performance of their learners.

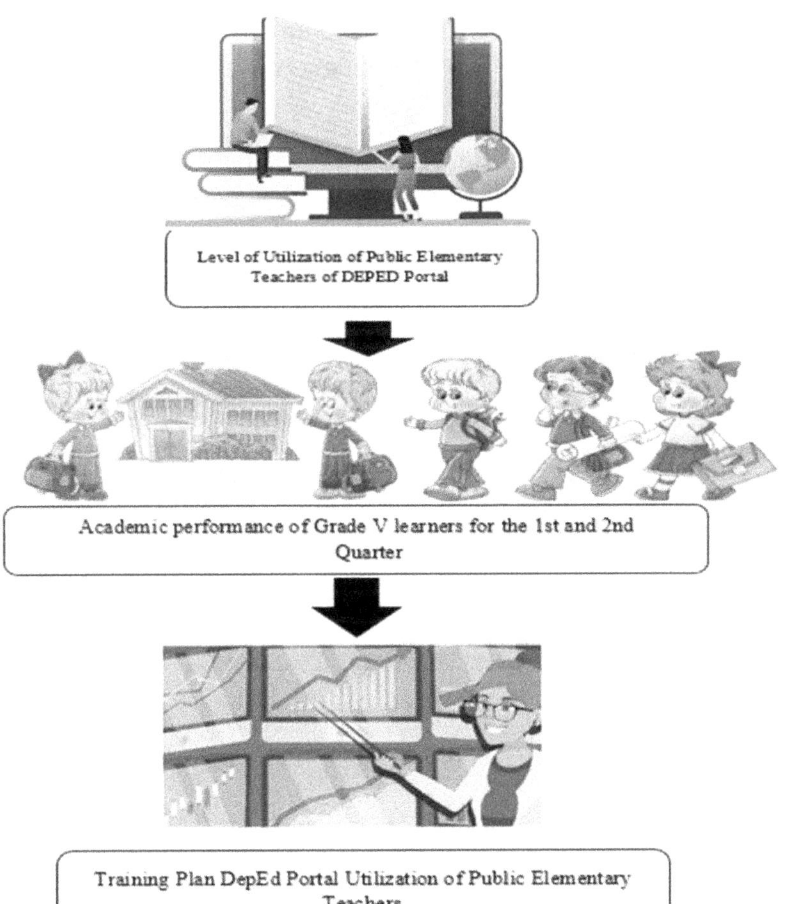

Figure 2: Conceptual Framework

Definition of Terms

The following terms are outlined operationally so as to own an improved understanding of the study:

DepEd Portal. This refers to the portal provided and by the Department of Education which is accessible for the teachers for utilization such as modules, worksheets, video lessons, daily lesson plan, and other learning materials that maid available for the welfare of teachers and learners.

LRMDS. Also known as Learning Resources Management and Development System that was created to ensure learning continuity designed by the Department of Education.

Student Learning Materials. Involves to the materials created by teachers and other experts in the field of education and uploaded to the DepEd Portal.

Teacher's Teaching Guide. This refers to the guide of teachers in delivering the lessons to the students.

TLMs. Also known as Teaching and Learning Materials that can be found in the DepEd Portal and made available for the utilization of teachers and learners.

Video Lessons. This pertains teachers' made video lessons that jive with the present curriculum and uploaded to the DepEd Portal for the utilization of teachers.

Chapter 3

RESEARCH DESIGN AND METHODOLOGY

This chapter presents the research design, the respondents, sampling techniques and instruments used for data gathering procedure and the statistical treatment of the data.

Research Design

Descriptive correlational research design method was used in this study because of its appropriateness to the topic of this research.

Furthermore, in scientific research, the descriptive correlational design refers to the sort of study in which data is collected without any alterations to the study's topic. It indicates that the experimenter cannot interact directly with the environment in which the experiment is being conducted in a way that would cause the experiment to change. A descriptive correlational study is one in which the researcher's primary goal is to describe correlations between variables rather than attempting to establish a causal link (McCombes, 2019). Further, this study will employ the descriptive correlational approach because the intention of this research is merely determining the level of DEPED portal utilization of public elementary teachers and academic performance of learners in selected public elementary schools in North II District, Division of Caloocan.

Respondents of thc Study

Since the study focused on determining the level of DEPED Portal Utilization of Public Elementary Teachers and Academic Performance of Learners in selected public elementary schools in North II District, Division of Caloocan during the School Year 2022-2023, the researcher collected data from one hundred (150) teachers from public elementary schools such as Bagong Silang Elementary School, Silanganan Elementary School, Kalayaan Elementary School, Gabriela Silang Elementary School, Sto. Nino Elemetary School and Rene Cayetano elementary School.

Sampling Technique

Quota sampling technique was used in selecting teacher-respondents. According to Economics Time (2020), quota sampling is a sampling methodology wherein data is collected from a homogeneous group. It involves a two-step process where two variables can be used to filter information from the population. It can easily be administered and helps in quick comparison. Quota sampling in the initial phases is a simple yet effective way of doing research. The researcher could select two variables from the population to study about a given group. The researcher might add additional sub-points to the data set according to the analysis requirements.

Research Instrument Used

The researcher utilized the following as measuring instruments in gathering and collecting the needed data:

□ Questionnaire

Respondents answered questions by checking the column that corresponds to their responses in the questionnaire provided by the researcher via Google Form. This was the primary source of data because it contained questions that will react to the Statement of the Problem in Chapter I. Some statements offer explanations for the respondent's attitude and point of view. A numerical value will be assigned to the responses, which was calculated using the relevant statistical instrument. The following are the parts of the questionnaire:

Part I: The level of utilization of public elementary teachers of DEPED portal as to Student Learning Materials, Teacher's Teaching Guide, and video lessons;

Part II: The Academic performance of Grade V learners for the 1st and 2nd Quarter; and

Part II: The challenges encountered and solutions offered in the utilization of DepEd Portal.

Validation of the Research Instrument

In the validation of the research instrument, the researcher assured that the adviser checked all the queries enclosed and requested suggestions for its improvement. When a series of revisions and changes, the teacher come up with the revision and wanted the approval of Thesis Committee. The researcher resents the draft to skilled for revision. All suggestions are reaching to be thought of in constructing the final word draft of the instruments. The questionnaires were distributed to 5 parent and 5 teachers for trial purposes to now if the questionnaires are appropriately address what is being asked in the Statement of the Problem. After the trial distribution of questionnaires, the researcher analyzed the questions and revised some words that the respondents recommended.

In addition, the researcher ensured that questionnaire will be validated by Master Teachers, Grade level chairmen, and LRMDS School Coordinator for ensuring that the instrument is valid and reliable and free from any prejudices.

Administration and Retrieval of the Questionnaires

The researcher sought authorization from the Caloocan City Schools Division Superintendent, District Supervisors, and elementary school principals in the North II District, Division of Caloocan. After receiving the approval letter which she presented to the school head of the selected schools to gather information from the respondents, the researcher personally administered the survey to the respondents using questionnaires. The link was sent to the teachers who responded. The researcher collected the questionnaires from the respondents after a week and they were consolidated, classified, organized and interpreted using the appropriate statistical tools.

The researcher guaranteed that the identity of respondents will be kept private. This is enshrined in Republic Act 10173, also known as the "Data Privacy Act of 2012," which states that the state's policy is to preserve the fundamental human right to privacy and communication while ensuring a free flow of information to stimulate innovation and growth.

Statistical Treatment of Data

After having retrieved the questionnaire, the data were tallied, encoded and tabulated, then statistically treated using the following tools:

Weighted Mean and Ranking - these statistical tools were used to answer questions number 1, and 5 in the statement of the problem stated in chapter 1. These tools were used to determine the level of utilization of Public Elementary Teachers of DEPED portal as assess by Master Teachers, Grade Level Chairman, and themselves. It also determines the challenges encountered and solution offered in the utilization of DEPED portal.

T-test – this statistical tool answers the second question of the statement of the problem stated in the first chapter. It is used to determine the significant difference in the assessment of the two group of respondents on the level of utilization of DEPED portal.

Frequency and Percentage - these descriptive statistical tools were used to determine the academic performance of Grade 5 learners for the first and second quarters based on the General Weighted Average (GWA). These tools also addressed questions number 3 of the statement of the problem stated in chapter one.

Spearman - rank Coefficient Correlation - This statistical tool answer question number 4 in the statement of the problem stated in chapter 1. It is used to determine the significant relationship between the level of DEPED portal utilization of the respondents and the academic performance of the learners in the first and second quarter.

Chapter 4

DATA PRESENTATION, ANALYSIS AND INTERPRETATION

This chapter presents the analysis, interpretation and discussion of the results of gathered information on the DepEd Portal utilization of public elementary teachers and academic performance of learners.

Findings are hereby revealed by presenting statistical tables to answer each question presented in the statement of the problems of the study.

1. The level of utilization of Public Elementary Teachers of DEPED portal as asses by Master Teachers, Grade Level Chairman, and themselves.

The level of utilization of Public Elementary Teachers of DEPED portal as asses by Master Teachers, Grade Level Chairman, and themselves as to Student Learning Materials, Teacher's Teaching Guide, and Video Lessons is shown in tables 1-4.

Table 1. The level of utilization of Public Elementary Teachers of DepEd portal as asses by Master Teachers, Grade and themselves in Terms of Student Learning Materials

Indicators	Teachers		Master Teachers		Grade Level Chairman				
	W.M.	**DV**	**W.M.**	**DV**	**W.M.**	**DV**	AWM	**DV**	**RANK**
1. Browse and download published resources intended for learners.	3.55	HU	3.55	HU	3.17	U	3.42	U	8

2. Accessing LRMDS website (http://www.lrmds.deped.gov.ph/).	3.48	U	3.20	U	3.58	HU	3.42	U	8
3. Finding and selecting learning Resources in the K – 12 Ladder	3.51	HU	3.70	HU	3.67	HU	3.63	HU	3
4. Downloading Learning Resources.	3.53	HU	3.85	HU	3.42	HU	3.60	HU	5
5. Using the downloaded resources as teaching and learning materials.	3.37	U	4.00	HU	4.00	HU	3.79	HU	1
6. Using the downloaded resources references / supplementary materials.	3.40	U	3.40	HU	3.83	HU	3.54	HU	6
7. Sharing the downloaded resources to others as teaching and learning materials.	3.42	U	3.85	HU	4.00	HU	3.76	HU	2
8. Sharing the downloaded resources to others as references/ supplementary materials.	3.43	U	2.85	U	3.92	HU	3.40	U	10
9. Teachers always download materials they used in their everyday TL process.	3.51	HU	3.55	HU	3.83	HU	3.63	HU	3
10. Materials downloaded in the portal fit the kind of learners and objectives of the lesson.	3.68	HU	3.25	U	3.58	HU	3.50	HU	7
Composite Weighted Mean	3.49	U	3.52	HU	3.70	HU	3.57	HU	

Legend: 4-Highly Utilized (HU) 3.50 - 4.00, 3-Utilized (U) 2.50 - 3.49, 2-Slightly Utilized (SU) 1.50 - 2.49, 1-Not Utilized (NU)1.00 - 1.49

On the Level of utilization of Public Elementary teachers of DEPED portal as assessed by Respondents in terms of Student Learning materials the indicator "Using the downloaded resources as teaching and learning materials" garnered

the highest average weighted mean of 3.79 with descriptive value of Highly Utilized, followed by "Sharing the downloaded resources to others as teaching and learning materials" with an average weighted mean of 3.76 and with descriptive value of Highly Utilized. “Finding and selecting learning resources in the K-12 ladder” and “Teachers always download materials they used in their everyday TL process” have identical average weighted mean of 3.63 and share the same rank with descriptive value of Highly Utilized.

Meanwhile, “Sharing the downloaded resources to others as references/supplementary materials” garnered the lowest weighted mean of 3.40 and a descriptive value of "Utilized". Overall, the average weighted mean of all the indicators is 3.57 with a descriptive value of Highly Utilized.

According to a study by Villanueva, Dela Cruz, and Espiritu (2021), teachers who frequently use the DEPED portal are more likely to have improved student learning outcomes. The study also discovered that teachers who used the portal felt more self-sufficient in their instructional strategies. In addition, Aquino and De Castro's (2021) also revealed that teachers who frequently used the DEPED portal had a better comprehension of the curriculum and were more likely to employ a variety of instructional tactics. The study concluded that the portal had a beneficial influence on the instructional strategies used by Filipino public elementary school instructors.

Finally, Garcia and Angeles (2021) investigated the extent to which teachers in the Philippines' rural regions used the DEPED portal. According to the study, even though some teachers had trouble using the portal because of their poor internet access, those who were able to utilize it frequently had a beneficial influence on student learning outcomes.

Table 2. Level of utilization of Public Elementary teachers of DepEd portal as assessed by Respondents in terms of Teachers Teaching Guide

Indicators Teachers Master Teachers Grade Level Chairman									
	W.M.	**DV**	**W.M.**	**DV**	**W.M.**	**DV**	AWM	DV	**RANK**
1. Browse and download published resources intended for teacher's teaching guide.	3.27	U	3.85	HU	3.83	HU	3.65	HU	3
2. Accessing LRMDS website (http://www.lrmds.deped.gov.ph/).	3.23	U	3.40	U	3.67	HU	3.43	U	9
3. Finding and selecting teacher's teaching guide for all subjects.	3.36	U	3.50	HU	3.92	HU	3.59	HU	6
4. Downloading teacher's teaching guide for all the subject assigned to the teachers.	3.41	U	3.15	U	3.75	3.58	HU	U	10
5. Using the downloaded teacher's teaching guide as Guide in making Daily Lesson Plan.	3.71	HU	3.40	U	3.75	HU	3.62	HU	4
6. Using the downloaded teacher's teaching guide as guide in making instructional materials.	3.70	HU	3.45	U	3.67	HU	3.61	HU	5
7. Sharing the downloaded teacher's teaching guide as guide in making Daily Lesson Plan.	3.65	HU	3.85	HU	3.83	HU	3.78	HU	1
8. Sharing the downloaded teacher's teaching guide as guide in making instructional materials.	3.75	HU	3.70	HU	3.75	HU	3.73	HU	2
9. The portal serves a teachers' guide in planning the lessons.	3.75	HU	3.35	U	3.58	HU	3.49	HU	8
10.Teachers utilizes the portal in planning the appropriate IM for the lessons they will tackle during their TL process.	3.61	HU	3.70	HU	3.25	U	3.52	HU	7
Composite Weighted Mean	**3.52**	HU	3.54	HU	3.68	HU	3.58	HU	

Legend:4 Highly Utilized (HU) 3.50 - 4.00, 3-Utilized (U) 2.50 - 3.49, 2-Slightly Utilized (SU) 1.50 - 2.49, 1-Not Utilized (NU)1.00 - 1.49

On the Level of utilization of Public Elementary teachers of DEPED portal as assessed by Respondents in terms of Teachers Teaching Guide the indicator “Sharing the downloaded teacher’s teaching guide as guide in making Daily Lesson Plan” garnered the highest weighted mean of 3.78 with descriptive value of Highly Utilized. Followed by “The portal serves a teachers’ guide in planning the lessons” with an average weighted mean of 3.73 with descriptive value of Highly Utilized. Next in rank is the indicator “Browse and download published resources intended for teacher’s teaching guide” with weighted mean of 3.65 with descriptive value of Highly Utilized.

Meanwhile, “Downloading teacher’s teaching guide for all the subject assigned to the teachers" garnered the lowest weighted mean of 3.38 and a descriptive value of "Utilized". Overall, the average weighted mean of all the indicators is 3.58 with a descriptive value of "Highly Utilized".

According to a research by Gomez and Acosta (2021), teachers who consistently use the DEPED site teaching guides are more likely to have lesson plans and classroom management techniques that are effective. The study also discovered that teachers who used the portal felt more confident in their instructional strategies.

Additionally, a research by Aguirre and Valdez (2021) indicated that teachers had access to a variety of teaching resources through the DEPED site, including lesson plans, exercises, and assessments that improved their teaching skills. The survey also discovered that teachers who used the portal felt more effective in their instruction. Finally, a research by Baluyot and Cayetano (2021) investigated the extent to which teachers in various parts of the Philippines used the DEPED online teaching guidelines.

Table 3. Level of utilization of Public Elementary teachers of DepEd portal as assessed by Respondents in terms of Video Lessons

Indicators	Teachers		Master Teachers		Grade Level Chairman				
	W.M.	**DV**	**W.M.**	**DV**	**W.M.**	**DV**	AWM	DV	**RANK**
1.Browse and download video lessons.	3.39	U	3.95	HU	3.58	HU	3.64	HU	6
2. Accessing LRMDS website (http://www.lrmds.deped.gov.ph/).	3.57	HU	3.80	HU	3.75	HU	3.71	HU	5
3. Finding and selecting video lessons for all subjects	3.73	HU	3.60	HU	3.92	HU	3.75	HU	2
4. Downloading video lessons for all the subject assigned to the teachers.	3.66	HU	3.85	HU	3.00	U	3.50	HU	7
5. Using the downloaded video lessons for instructional materials.	3.52	HU	4.00	HU	3.83	HU	3.78	HU	1
6. Using the downloaded video as basis in making Daily Lesson Plan or DLP.	3.45	U	3.70	HU	3.25	U	3.47	U	8
7. Sharing the downloaded video lessons for instructional materials.	3.29	U	3.90	HU	4.00	HU	3.73	HU	3
8. Sharing the downloaded video as basis in making Daily Lesson Plan.	3.75	HU	3.75	HU	3.67	HU	3.72	HU	4
9. Video lessons uploaded to the portal can easily access due to friendly-user									

apps of the portal.	3.30	U	2.95	U	2.75	U	3.00	U	10
10.Lessons become easier to generate due to the presence of video lessons that easily understand by the learners and teachers.	3.54	HU	3.80	HU	2.67	U	3.34	U	9
Composite Weighted Mean	**3.52**	HU	**3.73**	HU	**3.44**	HU	**3.56**	HU	

Legend:4-Highly Utilized (HU) 3.50 - 4.00, 3-Utilized (U) 2.50 - 3.49, 2-Slightly Utilized (SU) 1.50 - 2.49, 1-Not Utilized (NU) 1.00 - 1.49

On the Level of utilization of Public Elementary teachers of DepEd portal as assessed by Respondents in terms of Video Lessons. "Browse and download video lessons" garnered the highest weighted mean of 3.78 with descriptive value of Highly Utilized. Followed by "Finding and selecting video lessons for all subjects" with an average weighted mean of 3.75 with descriptive value of Highly Utilized. Next in rank is " Sharing the downloaded video lessons for instructional materials" with weighted mean of 3.73 with descriptive value of Highly Utilized.

Meanwhile, "Video lessons uploaded to the portal can easily access due to friendly-user apps of the portal" garnered the lowest weighted mean of 3.00 and with a descriptive value of "Utilized". Overall, the average weighted mean of all the indicators is 3.56 with a descriptive value of "Highly Utilized".

According to a research by Reyes and Garcia (2021), educators who frequently used the video courses on the DepEd portal were able to incorporate multimedia resources into their lesson plans. The survey also discovered that teachers who used the portal felt more effective in their instruction. Similar to this, a study by Garcia and Cortez (2021) revealed that teachers were able to create more interactive and interesting lessons for their students when they frequently used the DEPED site video lessons. The study concluded that the portal had a beneficial influence on the instructional strategies used by Filipino public elementary school instructors. In addition, a study by Fernandez and Reyes (2021) discovered that teachers had access to a variety of multimedia resources through the

DEPED portal video lessons, which improved their teaching methods. The study also discovered that instructors who made use of the portal had a better grasp of how to incorporate video courses into their pedagogical strategies.

Finally, a research by Ramos and Flores (2021) investigated the extent to which teachers in various parts of the Philippines used the DepEd online video lessons. According to the study, instructors who had access to the portal video lessons could provide their students more varied and engaging learning opportunities.

Table 4. Summary of Level of utilization of Public Elementary teachers of DepEd portal as assessed by the respondents

	Respondents							
	Teachers		**Master Teachers**		**Grade Chairmen**		**AWM**	**DV**
DEPED Portal	**W.M.**	**DV**	**W.M.**	**DV**	**W.M.**	**DV**		
Students Learning Materials	3.49	U	3.52	HU	3.70	HU	3.57	HU
Teacher's Teaching Guide	3.52	HU	3.54	HU	3.68	HU	3.58	HU
Video Lessons	3.52	HU	3.73	HU	3.44	U	3.56	HU
Overall WM	3.51	HU	3.60	HU	3.61	HU	3.57	HU

Table 4 presents summary of level of utilization of public elementary teachers of DipEd portal as assessed by the respondents. The Teacher's Teaching Guide has the highest average weighted mean of 3.58 and rank first among the indicators. It was followed by Students Learning Materials with an average weighted mean of 3.57 and rank second. The lowest rank among the indicators is Video Lessons with an average weighted mean of 3.57 and a descriptive value of "Highly Utilized". Overall, the average weighted mean of all the indicators is 3.57 with a descriptive value of "Highly Utilized".

2. Test of significant difference on the assessment of the two groups of respondents on the level of utilization of DepEd Portal when the aforementioned variables are considered.

The summary of the results of the test of significant difference on the assessment of the two groups of respondents on the level of utilization of DepEd Portal when the aforementioned variables are considered is shown in table 5. The decision whether to accept or reject the null hypothesis is set at the p-value of 0.05. All p-values equal to or greater than 0.05 leads to the acceptance while those lesser than 0.05 leads to the rejection of the null hypothesis.

Table 5. Test of significant difference on the assessment of the two groups of respondents on the level of utilization of DepEd Portal when Student Learning Materials, Teacher's Teaching Guide, and Video Lessons are considered.

Variables	**Computed t**	**Critical t .05.**	**Decision**	**Interpretation**
1 Student Learning Materials	0.27610	1.9431	Accept Ho	Not Significant
2.Teachers' Teaching Guide	1.11175	1.9431	Accept Ho	Not Significant
3 Video Lessons	0.16071	1.9431	Accept Ho	Not Significant

Table 5 presents the significant difference on the level of utilization of DEPED portal as assessed by the group of respondents. Based on the table, the absolute computed t-value of 0.27610 and critical t of 1.9431 for student learning materials, t- value of 1.11175 and critical t of 1.9431 for teacher's teaching guide, and t-value of 0.16071 and critical t of 1.9431 for video lessons are all less than the tabular that made the null hypothesis (Ho) rejected. This means that there is a significant difference in the assessment of the respondents in the level of utilization of DepEd portal. This further indicates that there is a significant difference in the assessment of the two groups of respondents or the assessment of the three groups are all different.

In the Philippines, Reyes and colleagues (2022) investigated the disparities in use levels between urban and rural schools. In comparison to rural schools, the survey indicated that urban schools used the portal more frequently. Nevertheless, the study also discovered that student performance was positively connected with utilization levels, regardless of whether the school was situated in an urban or rural area.

The researchers looked at the disparities in utilization levels between male and female teachers in the Philippines in a study by Santos and colleagues (2022). In particular, female teachers used the portal's teaching aids and video lectures at higher rates than male teachers, according to the survey.

3. The Academic performance of Grade 5 learners for the 1st and 2nd Quarter based on General Weighted Average (GWA).

The next tables show the Academic performance of Grade 5 learners for the 1st and 2nd Quarter based on General Weighted Average (GWA).

Table 6. Learners of School A

Student	1st Quarter		2nd Quarter		Average	
	Grades	DR	Grades	DR	Grades	DR
1	84	S	86	VS	85	VS
2	80	S	85	VS	83	S
3	81	S	84	S	83	S
4	83	S	85	VS	84	S
5	83	S	86	VS	85	VS
6	82	S	85	VS	84	S
7	83	S	84	S	84	S
8	85	VS	85	VS	85	VS
9	80	S	83	S	82	S
10	82	S	85	VS	84	S
11	83	S	83	S	83	S
12	82	S	86	VS	84	S
13	82	S	84	S	83	S
14	82	S	85	VS	84	S
15	83	S	86	VS	85	VS
16	83	S	84	S	84	S
17	82	S	84	S	83	S
18	86	VS	88	VS	87	VS
19	80	S	82	S	81	S
20	85	VS	84	S	85	VS
21	82	S	85	VS	84	S
22	80	S	85	VS	83	S
23	80	S	83	S	82	S
24	80	S	82	S	81	S
25	80	S	83	S	82	S

26	83	S	87	VS	85	VS
27	80	S	82	S	81	S
28	83	S	87	VS	85	VS
29	81	S	84	S	83	S
30	85	VS	88	VS	87	VS

Legend: O-Outstanding: 90-100 (Passed), VS-Very Satisfactory: 85- - 89 (Passed), S-Satisfactory: 0-84 (Passed) F-Fairly Satisfactory: 75-79 (Passed), D-Did not meet Expectations: Below 75 (Failed)

Grading Scale	First Grading		Second Grading		**Overall**		
	f	%	f	%	f	%	**Descriptive Rating**
90 – 100	0	0.00	0	0.00	0	0.00	Outstanding
85 – 89	4	13.33	16	53.33	9	30.00	Very satisfactory
80 – 84	26	86.67	14	46.67	21	70.00	Satisfactory
75 – 79	0	0.00	0	0.00	0	0.00	Fairly satisfactory
Below 75	0	0.00	0	0.00	0	0.00	Did not met Expectations
Total	**30**	**100%**	**30**	**100%**	**30**	**100%**	

The table 6 shows the academic performance of Grade 5 learners for the first and second quarter based on General Weighted Average (GWA).

For the school A, Student 18 and 30 got the highest average grade of 87% with descriptive rating of "Very Satisfactory". Followed by students 1, 2,18, 15,20 and 18 with average grade of 85% with a descriptive rating of "Very Satisfactory". Next, students 4,6,7,10,12,14 and 21 with average grade of 84% with a descriptive rating of "Satisfactory". Meanwhile, Students 27 and 19 got the lowest average grade of 81% with descriptive rating of "Satisfactory".

Overall, there are 9 out of 30 or 30% learners whose average grade is from 85 - 89 with a descriptive value of "Very Satisfactory".

Twenty-one out of thirty or 70% of the learners whose average grade is from 80 – 84. No learner has an average grade in the two quarters from 90 to 100 and below 75% whose descriptive value are "Outstanding", and "Did not meet expectations" respectively.

Table 7. Learners of School B

Student	1st Quarter		2nd Quarter		Average	
	Grades	DR	Grades	DR	Grades	DR
1	83	S	84	S	84	S
2	84	S	86	VS	85	VS
3	82	S	84	S	83	S
4	82	S	83	S	83	S
5	85	VS	87	VS	86	VS
6	85	VS	86	VS	86	VS
7	84	S	88	VS	86	VS
8	84	S	85	VS	85	VS
9	86	VS	88	VS	87	VS
10	84	S	85	VS	85	VS
11	85	VS	85	VS	85	VS
12	83	S	85	VS	84	S
13	82	S	84	S	83	S
14	81	S	82	S	82	S
15	86	VS	87	VS	87	VS
16	85	VS	86	VS	86	VS
17	83	S	85	VS	84	S
18	84	S	86	VS	85	VS
19	83	S	84	S	84	S
20	82	S	84	S	83	S
21	84	S	85	VS	85	VS
22	83	S	85	VS	84	S
23	83	S	85	VS	84	S
24	84	S	86	VS	85	VS
25	85	VS	87	VS	86	VS
26	82	S	84	S	83	S
27	82	S	84	S	84	S
28	84	S	85	VS	85	VS
29	85	VS	87	VS	86	VS
30	83	S	84	S	84	S
31	84	S	86	VS	85	VS
32	83	S	84	S	84	S
33	83	S	84	S	83	S
34	85	VS	86	VS	86	VS
35	86	VS	88	VS	87	VS
36	82	S	85	VS	84	S
37	83	S	85	VS	84	S
38	84	S	85	VS	85	VS
39	84	S	86	VS	85	VS
40	81	S	83	S	82	S

Legend: O-Outstanding: 90-100 (Passed), VS-Very Satisfactory: 85- - 89 (Passed), S-Satisfactory: 0-84 (Passed)
F-Fairly Satisfactory: 75-79 (Passed), D-Did not meet Expectations: Below 75 (Failed)

Grading Scale	First Grading		Second Grading		Overall		Descriptive Rating
	f	%	f	%	f	%	
90 – 100	0	0.00	0	0.0 0	0	0.00	Outstanding
85 – 89	10	25.00	27	67.50	21	52.50	Very satisfactory
80 – 84	30	75.00	13	32.50	19	47.50	Satisfactory
75 – 79	0	0.00	0	0.00	0	0.00	Fairly Satisfactory
Below 75	0	0.00	0	0.00	0	0.00	Did not met Expectations
Total	**40**	**100%**	**40**	**100%**	**40**	**100%**	

The table 7 For the school B, student 9 ,15 and 35 got the highest average grade of 87% with descriptive rating of “Very Satisfactory”. Followed by students 5, 6, 16, 25, 29 and 34 with average grade of 85% with descriptive rating of “Very Satisfactory”. Eleven out 40 students got an average rating of 85% with descriptive rating “Very satisfactory” and rank third. Meanwhile, Student 14 and 40 got the lowest average grade of 80% with descriptive rating of “Satisfactory”.

Overall, there are 21 out of 40 or 30% learners whose average grade is from 85 - 89 with a descriptive value of "Very Satisfactory".

Nineteen out of forty or 70% of the learners whose average grade is from 80 – 84 with a descriptive value of "Satisfactory". No learner has an average grade in the two quarters from 90 to 100 and below 75% whose descriptive value are "Outstanding", and "Did not meet expectations" respectively.

Table 8. Learners of School C

Student	1st Quarter		2nd Quarter		Average	
	Grades	**DR**	**Grades**	**DR**	**Grades**	**DR**
1	86	VS	87	VS	87	VS
2	80	S	80	S	80	S
3	81	S	84	S	83	S
4	82	S	85	VS	84	S
5	82	S	85	VS	84	S
6	82	S	83	S	83	S
7	80	S	84	S	82	S
8	80	S	82	S	81	S
9	80	S	81	S	81	S
10	84	S	87	VS	86	VS
11	84	S	85	VS	85	VS
12	80	S	80	S	80	S
13	82	S	84	S	83	S
14	81	S	82	S	82	S
15	80	S	82	S	81	S
16	79	F	81	S	80	S
17	82	S	82	S	82	S
18	81	S	82	S	82	S
19	79	F	83	S	81	S
20	83	S	84	S	84	S
21	83	S	84	S	84	S
22	82	S	84	S	83	S
23	80	S	80	S	80	S
24	78	F	81	S	80	S
25	81	S	82	S	82	S
26	83	S	83	S	83	S
27	81	S	84	S	83	S
28	83	S	84	S	84	S
29	81	S	83	S	82	S
30	79	F	82	S	81	S
31	79	F	81	S	80	S
32	82	S	83	S	83	S
33	83	S	84	S	84	S
34	84	S	86	VS	85	VS
35	80	S	80	S	80	S
36	83	S	85	VS	84	S
37	82	S	83	S	83	S
38	83	S	84	S	84	S
39	79	F	81	S	80	S
40	82	S	85	VS	84	S

Legend: O-Outstanding: 90-100 (Passed), VS-Very Satisfactory: 85- - 89 (Passed), S-Satisfactory: 0-84 (Passed) F-Fairly Satisfactory: 75-79 (Passed), D-Did not meet Expectations: Below 75 (Failed)

Grading Scale	First Grading f	%	Second Grading f	%	**Overall** f	%	**Descriptive Rating**
90 – 100	0	0.00	0	0.00	0	0.00	Outstanding
85 – 89	0	0.00	7	17.50	3	7.50	Very satisfactory

80 – 84	34	85.00	33	82.50	37	92.50	Satisfactory
75 – 79	6	15.00	0	0.00	0	0.00	Fairly satisfactory
Below 75	0	0.00	0	0.00	0	0.00	Did not met Expectations
Total	**40**	**100%**	**40**	**100%**	**40**	**100%**	

Table 8 For the school C, student 1 got the highest average grade of 87% with descriptive rating of "Very Satisfactory". Followed by student 10 with the average grade of 86% with descriptive rating of "Very Satisfactory". Next are students 11 and 34 with the average grade of 85% with descriptive rating of "Very Satisfactory". And students 12, 16, 23, 24, 31, 35 and 39 got the lowest average grade of 80% with descriptive rating of "Satisfactory".

Overall, there are 3 out of 40 or 7.50% learners whose average grade is from 85 - 89 with a descriptive value of "Very Satisfactory".

Thirty-seven out of forty or 92.50% of the learners whose average grade is from 80 – 84 with a descriptive value of "Satisfactory". No learner has an average grade in the two quarters from 90 to 100 and below 75% whose descriptive value are "Outstanding", and "Did not meet expectations" respectively.

Table 9. Learners of School D

Student	1st Quarter		2nd Quarter		Average	
	Grades	DR	Grades	DR	Grades	DR
1	81	S	84	S	83	S
2	78	F	82	S	80	S
3	82	S	83	S	83	S
4	82	S	84	S	83	S
5	82	S	84	S	83	S
6	83	S	85	VS	84	S
7	81	S	84	S	83	S
8	81	S	83	S	82	S
9	81	S	83	S	82	S
10	81	S	84	S	83	S
11	84	S	86	VS	85	VS
12	80	S	83	S	82	S
13	84	S	86	VS	85	VS
14	81	S	84	S	83	S
15	80	S	84	S	82	S
16	80	S	83	S	82	S
17	82	S	84	S	83	S
18	81	S	83	S	82	S
19	80	S	82	S	81	S

20	79	F	81	S	80	S
21	79	F	80	S	80	S
22	80	S	81	S	81	S
23	81	S	84	S	83	S
24	81	S	83	S	82	S
25	84	S	86	VS	85	VS
26	81	S	84	S	83	S
27	85	VS	87	VS	86	VS
28	82	S	85	VS	84	S
29	79	F	81	S	80	S
30	80	S	83	S	82	S
31	84	S	86	VS	85	VS
32	85	VS	86	VS	86	VS
33	83	S	85	VS	84	S
34	79	F	80	S	80	S
35	85	VS	87	VS	86	VS
36	84	S	86	VS	85	VS
37	84	S	86	VS	85	VS
38	80	S	84	S	82	S
39	82	S	84	S	83	S
40	84	S	86	VS	85	VS
41	84	S	85	VS	85	VS
42	85	VS	87	VS	86	VS
43	83	S	84	S	82	S
44	80	S	84	S	82	S
45	79	F	82	S	81	S

Legend: O-Outstanding: 90-100 (Passed), VS-Very Satisfactory: 85- - 89 (Passed), S-Satisfactory: 0-84 (Passed) F-Fairly Satisfactory: 75-79 (Passed), D-Did not meet Expectations: Below 75 (Failed)

	First Grading		Second Grading		**Overall**		
Grading Scale	f	%	f	%	f	%	**Descriptive Rating**
90 – 100	0	0.00	0	0.00	0	0.00	Outstanding
85 – 89	0	0.00	7	17.50	3	7.50	Very satisfactory
80 – 84	34	85.00	33	82.50	37	92.50	Satisfactory
75 – 79	6	15.00	0	0.00	0	0.00	Fairly satisfactory
Below 75	0	0.00	0	0.00	0	0.00	Did not met Expectations

For the school D, students 27 ,32, 35, and 42 got the highest average grade of 86%, with descriptive rating of “Very Satisfactory”. Followed by students 11, 25, 31, 36, 37, 40 and 41 with the average grade of 85% with descriptive rating of “Very Satisfactory. Next are students 6, 28 and 33 with an average grade of 84% with descriptive rating of “Satisfactory”.

Meanwhile, Students 2, 20, 21, 29 and 34 got the lowest average grade of 80% with descriptive rating of "Satisfactory".

Overall, there are 12 out of 45 or 26.67% learners whose average grade is from 85 - 89 with a descriptive value of "Very Satisfactory".

Thirty-three out of forty-five or 73.33% of the learners whose average grade is from 80 – 84 with a descriptive value of "Satisfactory". No learner has an average grade in the two quarters from 90 to 100 and below 75% whose descriptive value are "Outstanding", and "Did not meet expectations" respectively.

Table 10. Learners of School E

Student	1st Quarter		2nd Quarter		Average	
	Grades	**DR**	**Grades**	**DR**	**Grades**	**DR**
1	86	VS	88	VS	87	VS
2	85	VS	87	VS	86	VS
3	83	S	85	VS	84	S
4	85	VS	86	VS	86	VS
5	84	S	85	VS	85	VS
6	86	VS	87	VS	87	VS
7	84	S	86	VS	85	VS
8	85	VS	87	VS	86	VS
9	83	S	85	VS	84	S
10	81	S	84	S	83	S
11	83	S	85	VS	84	S
12	82	S	84	S	83	S
13	84	S	85	VS	85	VS
14	85	VS	86	VS	86	VS
15	85	VS	87	VS	86	VS
16	86	VS	87	VS	87	VS
17	86	VS	88	VS	87	VS
18	85	VS	87	VS	86	VS
19	84	S	86	VS	85	VS
20	84	S	85	VS	85	VS
21	83	S	85	VS	84	S
22	84	S	85	VS	85	VS
23	85	VS	87	VS	86	VS
24	84	S	86	VS	85	VS
25	85	VS	88	VS	87	VS
26	84	S	87	VS	86	VS
27	85	VS	88	VS	87	VS
28	86	VS	89	VS	88	VS
29	83	S	85	VS	84	S
30	84	S	86	VS	85	VS
31	85	VS	87	VS	86	VS
32	85	VS	88	VS	87	VS
33	84	S	87	VS	86	VS
34	83	S	85	VS	84	S
35	86	VS	88	VS	87	VS
36	85	VS	87	VS	86	VS

37	86	VS	88	VS	87	VS
38	83	S	85	VS	84	S
39	85	VS	87	VS	86	VS
40	85	VS	87	VS	86	VS
41	84	S	85	VS	85	VS
42	85	VS	86	VS	84	S
43	86	VS	87	VS	87	VS
44	84	S	85	VS	85	VS
45	86	VS	89	VS	88	VS

Legend: O-Outstanding: 90-100 (Passed), VS-Very Satisfactory: 85- - 89 (Passed), S-Satisfactory: 0-84 (Passed) F-Fairly Satisfactory: 75-79 (Passed), D-Did not meet Expectations: Below 75 (Failed)

Grading Scale	First Grading		Second Grading		**Overall**		**Descriptive Rating**
	%	**f**	**%**	**f**	**%**	**f**	
90 – 100		.00		.00		.00	Outstanding
85 – 89	4	3.33	3	5.56	5	7.78	Very satisfactory
80 – 84	1	6.67		.44	0	2.22	Satisfactory
75 – 79		.00		.00		.00	Fairly Satisfactory
Below 75		.00		.00		.00	Did not met Expectations
Total	**5**	**00%**	**5**	**00%**	**5**	**00%**	

For the school E, student 28 and 45 got the highest average grade of 88%, with descriptive rating of "Very Satisfactory". Followed by students 1,6,16,17,25,27,32,35,37, and 43 with the average grade of 87% with descriptive rating of "Very Satisfactory".

Next are students 2, 4, 8, 14, 15, 18, 23, 26, 31, 36, and 39 with the average of 86% with descriptive rating of "Very Satisfactory".

Meanwhile, Students 10 and 12 got the lowest grade of 83% with descriptive rating of "Satisfactory".

Overall, there are 35 out of 45 or 77.78% learners whose average grade is from 85 - 89 with a descriptive value of "Very Satisfactory".

Ten out of forty-five or 22.22% of the learners whose average grade is from 80 – 84 with a descriptive value of "Satisfactory". No learner has an average grade in the two quarters from 90 to 100 and below 75% whose descriptive value are "Outstanding", and "Did not meet expectations" respectively.

Grading Scale	First Grading f	%	Second Grading f	%	Overall f	%	Descriptive Rating
90 - 100	0	0.00	0	0.00	0	0.00	Outstanding
85 - 89	42	21.00	108	54.00	80	40.00	Very satisfactory
80 - 84	146	73.00	92	46.00	120	60.00	Satisfactory
75 - 79	12	6.00	0	0.00	0	0.00	Fairly Satisfactory
Below 75	0	0.00	0	0.00	0	0.00	Did not met Expectations
Total	200	100 %	200	100%	200	100 %	

Overall, there are 80 out of 200 or 40% learners whose average grade is from 85 - 89 with a descriptive value of "Very Satisfactory". One hundred twenty out of 200 or 60% of the learners whose average grade is from 80 – 84 with a descriptive value of "Satisfactory". No learner has an average grade in the two quarters from 90 to 100 and below 75% whose descriptive value are "Outstanding", and "Did not meet expectations" respectively.

According Fernandez and colleagues (2022) the learners' academic performance significantly improved between the first and second quarters, as evidenced by their GWA. The utilization of interactive teaching strategies and higher levels of student participation in the classroom were two of the aspects the researchers attributed to this development. Santos and colleagues (2022) conducted another study to examine the connection between students in grade 5's academic performance and the classroom environment. The study discovered a favorable correlation between academic achievement, as determined by the learners' GWA, and a pleasant classroom environment, which is characterized by positive student-teacher interactions and a safe and supportive learning environment. Researchers Tan and colleagues (2022) looked at the impact of student engagement on grade 5 students' academic achievement. According to the study, pupils who were more actively involved in their education performed better academically, as indicated by their GWA. The researchers proposed that interactive teaching strategies and chances for student-centered learning could foster more student involvement.

4. Test of significant relationship between the level of DepEd portal utilization and the academic performance of learners.

The significant relationship between the level of DepEd portal utilization and the academic performance of learners in table 12. Each verbal description has a corresponding scale on numerical values.

Table 11 Significant relationship between the level of DepEd portal utilization and the academic performance of the learners.

Level of DEPED Portal utilization	Correlation Coefficient (r)	Test Statistic (t)	Tabular Value	Decision	Interpretation VI
Student learning materials	0.127	0.363	± 2.262	Accept Ho	Not Significant
Teacher's teaching guide	-0.249	-0.726	± 2.262	Accept Ho	Not Significant
Video Lessons	0.746	3.163	± 2.262	Reject Ho	Not Significant

Table 11 presents the significant relationship between the level of DepEd portal utilization and the academic performance of grade 5 learners in the first and second quarters. Based on the table, the absolute computed t-value of 0.363 and

0.726 for student learning materials and teacher's teaching guide respectively are both less than the tabular value of 2.262, the null hypothesis will be accepted. This means that there is no significant relationship between the level of DepEd portal utilization and the academic performance of the learners.

On the contrary, the computed t-value of 3.163 for the DepEd portal video lessons is greater than the critical value of 2.262, the null hypothesis will be rejected in favor of the alternative hypothesis. This means that DepEd portal Utilization in terms of video lessons and the academic performance of the learners during the two quarters. This further indicates that if the teachers highly utilized the video lessons in the DepEd portal, the academic performance of the learners will get better and vice versa.

Access to a variety of educational resources, including student learning materials, teacher teaching aids, and video classes, is made possible by the DEPED portal. Numerous researches have been carried out to see if learners' use of the DEPED site is linked to improved academic performance. Cruz and colleagues (2022) conducted a study in which they looked at the connection between Filipino high school students' academic achievement and the use of the DEPED portal. The results of the study revealed a substantial positive link between the degree of DEPED portal usage and the students' grade-based academic performance. The DepEd site may be a beneficial tool for raising student academic performance, according to the researchers.

In addition, Garcia and colleagues (2022) looked at the connection between Filipino elementary school kids' academic achievement and DEPED portal usage in a different study. According to the study, DEPED portal users had greater academic performance levels, which showed up in their grades. The researchers recommended using the DEPED portal to give students access to top-notch learning resources that could improve their academic performance.

5. The challenges encountered and solution offered in the utilization of DepEd Portal.

The challenges encountered and solution offered in the utilization of DEDPED Portal is shown in table 12.

Table 12. The challenges encountered in the utilization of DepEd Portal

Challenges encountered and solution offered in the utilization of DEDPED Portal	W.M.	DV	Rank
1. The implementation of LRMDS requires the teachers more work, since they are the ones who will evaluate existing LRs and produce new ones.	3.01	E	10
2. There is no clear format in producing and evaluating different kinds of LRs.	3.06	E	9
3. Lacking of motivation for the teachers to produce an LR.	3.12	E	8
4. School does not have a stable connection.	3.44	E	3
5. Registration process is time-consuming.	3.45	E	2
6. Cannot access the portal because no accounts yet due to difficulty in creating one.	3.48	E	1
7. Difficulty in receiving confirmation from the Division Office if the account is accepted.	3.37	E	4
8. Lack or limited funding in producing LR.	3.23	E	7
9. Lack or limited coordination and cooperation of the important people.	3.36	E	5
10.Registering to the portal is time-consuming; signing-in, a hassle; and accessing the download portal, a difficulty.	3.33	E	6
Over-All Weighted Mean	3.29	E	

Legend:4-Highly Encountered (HE) 3.50-4.00, 3-Encountered (E) 2.50-3.49,2-Less Encountered (LE), 1.50 - 2.49, 1- Encountered (E) 1.00 - 1.49

Table 8 shows the challenges encountered by the respondents in the Utilization of DepEd portal. Based on the table, the indicator "Cannot access the portal because no accounts yet due to difficulty in creating one" whose weighted mean is 3.48 has the highest rank among the indicators. It was followed by "Registration process is time-consuming" with a weighted mean of 3.45 and rank second. Next to it is School does not have a stable connection" with a weighted mean of 3.44 and third rank among the challenges encountered.

The next three indicators are " Difficulty in receiving confirmation from the Division Office if the account is accepted.", "Lack or limited coordination and cooperation of the important people" and " Registering to the portal is time-consuming; signing-in, a hassle; and accessing the download portal, a difficulty" whose weighted mean are 3.37, 3.36, and 3.33 respectively. The seventh rank among the challenges is "Lack or limited funding in producing LR" whose weighted mean is 3.23. The last three indicators in the ranking are " Lacking of motivation for the teachers to produce an LR", "There is no clear format in producing and evaluating different kinds of LRs.", and "The implementation of LRMDS requires the teachers more work, since they are the ones who will evaluate existing LRs and produce new ones" whose weighted mean are 3.12 , 3.06 , and 3.01 respectively.

Overall, the average weighted mean of all the indicators is 3.29 and with a descriptive value of "Encountered". Since it gives access to a variety of learning resources that might improve students' academic performance, the DEPED (Department of Education) Portal has grown in popularity in recent years.

The DepEd Portal's use does present certain difficulties, though. To identify and investigate the difficulties users of the DepEd Portal confront, several researches have been carried out. Researchers Lim and colleagues (2022) looked at the difficulties teachers have using the DepEd Portal in one study. According to the survey, teachers faced a number of obstacles, including technical problems while trying to access and utilize the portal, a lack of instruction on how to use it, and restricted access to the required hardware and software.

The solutions offered in the utilization of DepEd Portal is shown in Table 13.

Table 13. The solutions offered in the utilization of DepEd Portal

Solutions offered in the utilization of DepEd Portal	W.M.	DV	Rank
1. Enhanced LRMDS adds, essentially, the digitalization of LRs to the 'old' LRMDS.	3.83	HR	10
2. Division offices should design a standard format to be used by all schools.	3.92	HR	9
3. Offering incentives for the teachers to motivate them to produce LRs.	3.96	HR	7
4. Funding of high speed internet connection.	3.98	HR	4
5. Reformat the registration process to avoid difficulty in doing so.	3.94	HR	8
6. Division offices should have personnel assigned to oversee the registration process of all coordinators.	3.97	HR	6
7. Ensure that all personnel assigned in LRMDS will be updated on the flor of confirmation of accounts to avoid delays.	3.99	HR	2
8. The school allot funds that will generate the creation of LR and sustaining the LR portals.	3.98	HR	4
9.The school head assigned teachers who will maintain the school portal and monitors their performance religiously	4.00	HR	1
10. Make the registration easier to motivate teachers to register in the portal. The more registrants, the more the LR portal become functional.	3.98	HR	4
Over-All Weighted Mean	3.96	HR	

Legend:4-Highly Recommended (HR) 3.50-4.00, 3-Recommended (R) 2.50-3.49, 2-Somewhat Recommended (SR) 1.50-2.49, 1-Not Recommended (NR) 1.00-1.49

Table 13 shows the solutions offered in the utilization of DepEd Portal. Based on the table, the indicator " The school head assigned teachers who will maintain the school portal and monitors their performance religiously" whose weighted mean is 4.00 has the highest rank among the indicators. It was followed by "Ensure that all personnel assigned in LRMDS will be updated on the flor of confirmation of accounts to avoid delays" with a weighted mean of 3.99 and rank second. Next to it are “Funding of high speed internet connection”, "The school allot funds that will generate the creation of LR and sustaining the LR portals” .and “Make the registration easier to motivate teachers to register in the portal. The more registrants, the more the LR portal become functional" with a weighted mean of 3.98 and third rank among the solutions offered.

The next three indicator is "Division offices should have personnel assigned to oversee the registration process of all coordinators", "Offering incentives for the teachers to motivate them to produce LRs" and "Reformat the registration process to avoid difficulty in doing so" whose weighted mean are 3.97, 3.96, and 3.94 respectively. The ninth rank among the solutions is "Division offices should design a standard format to be used by all schools" whose weighted mean is 3.92. The last rank among the indicators is "Enhanced LRMDS adds, essentially, the digitalization of LRs to the 'old' LRMDS." whose weighted mean are 3.83. Overall, the average weighted mean of all the indicators is 3.96 and with a descriptive value of "Highly Recommended".

In the Philippines, using the DepEd (Department of Education) Portal has become more crucial recently, especially in light of the COVID-19 pandemic. Although using the DepEd Portal has certain difficulties, numerous researches have been done to discover and consider potential solutions. In one study by Fernandez and colleagues (2022), the researchers put out a number of suggestions to deal with the difficulties users of the DepEd Portal encountered. The availability of hardware and software was increased, teachers, students, and parents received ongoing training, and the user-friendliness of the portal's interface was enhanced. Another study by Tan and colleagues (2022) looked into how well a teacher training program worked to improve how instructors used the DepEd Portal. The training session considerably increased instructors' knowledge of the portal and their capacity to usc it effectively in their instruction, according to the report.

A series of recommendations to assist parents in their children's use of the DepEd Portal were made in a study by Pascual and colleagues (2022). In accordance with these principles, parents should be given access to the essential gear and software, as well as constant communication between schools and parents.

TECHNOLOGICAL SKILLS FOR 20th CENTURY TEACHERS

By: CRISTINA B. TAAY

*Kindly see Appendix A

Chapter 5

SUMMARY OF FINDINGS, CONCLUSIONS AND RECOMMENDATIONS

This chapter discussed the summary of findings, conclusions and recommendations based on the analysis and interpretation presented in the preceding chapter.

Findings

The following are the summarized findings based on the computed data presented in the Chapter 4 of this study:

1. The level of utilization of Public Elementary Teachers of DepEd portal as asses by Master Teachers, Grade Level Chairman, and themselves

1.1. On the Student Learning Materials, the indicator "Using the downloaded resources as teaching and learning materials" garnered the highest average weighted mean of 3.79 with descriptive value of Highly Utilized, followed by "Sharing the downloaded resources to others as teaching and learning materials" with an average weighted mean of 3.76 and with descriptive value of Highly Utilized.

1.2. On Teachers Teaching Guide, the indicator "Sharing the downloaded teacher's teaching guide as guide in making Daily Lesson Plan" garnered the highest weighted mean of 3.78 with descriptive value of Highly Utilized. Followed by "The portal serves a teachers' guide in planning the lessons" with an average weighted mean of 3.73 with descriptive value of Highly Utilized. Next in rank is the indicator "Browse and download published resources intended for teacher's teaching guide" with weighted mean of 3.65 with descriptive value of Highly Utilized.

1.3 On the Level of utilization of Public Elementary teachers of DepEd portal as assessed by Respondents in terms of Video Lessons. "Browse and download video lessons" garnered the highest weighted mean of 3.78 with descriptive value of Highly Utilized. Followed by "Finding and selecting video lessons for all subjects" with an average weighted mean of 3.75 with descriptive value of Highly Utilized. Next in rank is " Sharing the downloaded video lessons for instructional materials" with weighted mean of 3.73 with descriptive value of Highly Utilized.

2. The absolute computed t-value of 0.27610 and critical t of 1.9431 for student learning materials, t- value of 1.11175 and critical t of 1.9431 for teacher's teaching guide, and t-value of 0.16071 and critical t of 1.9431 for video lessons are all less than the tabular that made the null hypothesis (Ho) rejected. This means that there is a significant difference in the assessment of the respondents in the level of utilization of DepEd portal.

3. Most of the students are averaging from 80-84 percent on their academic performance based on the average grade that gives them a descriptive value of Satisfactory.

4. The absolute computed t-value of 0.363 and 0.726 for student learning materials and teacher's teaching guide respectively are both less than the tabular value of 2.262, the null hypothesis will be accepted. This means that there is no significant relationship between the level of DepEd portal utilization and the academic performance of the learners. On the contrary, the computed t-value of 3.163 for the DepEd portal video lessons is greater than the critical value of 2.262, the null hypothesis will be rejected in favor of the alternative hypothesis.

5. On the challenges encountered in the utilization of DepEd Portal the indicator " Cannot access the portal because no accounts yet due to difficulty in creating one." whose weighted mean is 3.48 has the highest rank among the indicators, followed by " Registration process is time- consuming" with weighted mean of 3.45 and rank second and the third in rank is "School does not have a stable connection" with weighted mean of 3.44 and third rank among the challenges encountered.

The solutions offered in the utilization of DepEd Portal the indicator "The school head assigned teachers who will maintain the school portal and monitors their performance religiously", garnered the highest weighted mean of 4.00. Followed by "Ensure that all personnel assigned in LRMDS will be updated on the floor of confirmation of accounts to avoid delays", with a weighted mean of 3.99. Next to it are "Funding of high speed internet connection", "The school allot funds that will generate the creation of LR and sustaining the LR portals", and "Make the registration easier to motivate teachers to register in the portal. With a weighted mean of 3.98 and third rank among the solutions offered.

6. There is a proposed training plan based on the findings of the study.

Conclusions

The following are the conclusions formulated from the computed data presented in the Chapter 4 of this study:

1. The level of utilization of Public Elementary Teachers of DepEd portal as asses by Master Teachers, Grade Level Chairman, and themselves as to Student Learning Materials, Teacher's Teaching Guide, and Video Lessons are highly utilized by the respondents.
2. There is a significant difference in the assessment of the respondents in the level of utilization of DepEd portal. Therefore, the null hypothesis is rejected.
3. The Academic performance of Grade 5 learners increased from 1st to 2nd Quarter based on General Weighted Average (GWA). This further indicates that DepEd portal utilization is vital for enhancing learner's academic performance.
4. DepEd portal utilization in terms of video lessons and the academic performance of the learners during the two quarters. If the teachers highly utilized the video lessons in the DepEd portal, the academic performance of the learners will get better. Therefore, the null hypothesis is rejected.
5. The highly encountered challenges in the utilization of DepEd Portal are; "Cannot access the portal because no accounts yet due to

difficulty in creating one", "Registration process is time-consuming", and "School does not have a stable connection".

Wherein the solutions offered were "The school head assigned teachers who will maintain the school portal and monitors their performance religiously", " Ensure that all personnel assigned in LRMDS will be updated on the floor of confirmation of accounts to avoid delays", "Funding of high speed internet connection", "The school allot funds that will generate the creation of LR and sustaining the LR portals", and "Make the registration easier to motivate teachers to register in the portal. The more registrants, the more the LR portal become functional".

6. There is a proposed training plan for teachers based on the findings of the study entitled "Technological Skills for 20th Century Teachers".

Recommendations

On the account of conclusions presented in this study, the following recommendations are drawn:

1. The researcher highly encourages the teachers to continually utilize the DepEd portal for improving learners' academic performance among various technological learning materials. And conduct a comprehensive training to public elementary teachers on how to effectively utilize the DepEd portal for accessing student learning materials, teacher's teaching guides, and videos. This training should focus on maximizing the benefits of the portal in enhancing teaching and learning outcomes.

2. The researcher highly recommends public school administrators to assign dedicated personnel, to monitor the utilization of the DepEd portal. They should regularly assess the extent to which teachers are using the portal and provide support and guidance as needed. This monitoring process will ensure consistent utilization and identify any areas for improvement.

3. The researcher highly recommends to ensure that the DepEd Portal is updated regularly with relevant and accurate information that can support the teaching and learning process. This can include lesson

plans, assessment tools, and other resources that are aligned with the curriculum.

4. The researcher highly recommends to monitor the utilization of the DepEd Portal by public elementary teachers and track the academic performance of learners. This can help determine if there is a correlation between the two variables and if the portal is contributing to improved learning outcomes.

5. The researcher recommends to develop strategies to overcome the challenges faced by teachers in utilizing the DepEd portal. This may involve providing technical support, troubleshooting assistance, or additional training specifically addressing the identified challenges. Regularly communicate with teachers to understand their needs and concerns and implement appropriate solutions.

6. The researcher highly recommends for the adaptation and utilization of proposed training plan titled "Technological Skills for 21st Century Teachers" based on the study findings.

BIBLIOGRAPHY

Abendaño,K. D. (2020) The Role Of Pdos In Learning Resource Design And Development. https://www.depedmalaybalay.net/articles/the-role-of-pdos-in-learning-resource-design-and-development.html

Aguirre, M. P., & Valdez, J. P. (2021). The Utilization of the DEPED Portal Teaching Guides: Its Impact on the Teaching Practices of Public Elementary School Teachers in the Philippines. International Journal of Learning, Teaching and Educational Research, 20(4), 96-105.

Aquino, J. R. A., & De Castro, J. A. (2021). The Utilization of the DepEd Portal: Its Impact on the Teaching Practices of Public Elementary School Teachers in the Philippines. Journal of Educational Research, 3(3), 98-106.

Baluyot, A. S., & Cayetano, C. M. (2021). The Level of Utilization of DEPED Portal Teaching Guides by Public Elementary School Teachers in Different Regions of the Philippines. Journal of Education and Practice, 12(15), 101-110.

Chirwa, M. (2018). Access and use of internet in teaching and learning at two selected teachers' colleges in Tanzania. International Journal of Education and Development using Information and Communication Technology, 14(2), 4-16

Chi-Kin Lee, J. (2020). "Managing and Leading University Response to Support Psychosocial Health during COVID-19 Pandemic," in Webinar Series 2 in SEAMEO's Response to Pandemic COVID-19 (SEAMWO).

Cruz, J., et al. (2022). DEPED Portal Utilization and Academic Performance among High School Students in the Philippines. Journal of Education and Practice, 13(3), 45-58.

Dayagbil FT, Palompon DR, Garcia LL and Olvido MMJ (2021) Teaching and Learning Continuity Amid and Beyond the

Pandemic. Front. Educ. 6:678692. doi: 10.3389/feduc.2021.678692

DepEd Tambayan (2021) 2021 DepEd LRMDS Portal. https://depedtambayan.net/lrmds-portal/

DM 82, s. 2017 – Learning Resource Management and Development System Implementation in the Rationalized DepEd Structure

DO 35, s. 2010. Uploading of Sample Learning Resource Materials through the Learning Resources Management and Development System (LRMDS)

Edizon, F. (2020). Rewiring Higher Education in the Time of COVID-19 and beyond.

Fernandez, L. A., & Reyes, M. C. (2021). The Utilization of the DEPED Portal Video Lessons: Its Impact on the Teaching Practices of Public Elementary School Teachers in the Philippines. International Journal of Learning, Teaching and Educational Research, 20(3), 105-114.

Fernandez, R., et al. (2022). Academic Performance of Grade 5 Learners in the First and Second Quarters Based on General Weighted Average. Journal of Education and Practice, 13(2), 25-38.

Fernandez, R., et al. (2022). Solutions to Challenges Encountered in the Utilization of the DEPED Portal. Journal of Education and Practice, 13(4), 20-35.

Hijazi, S. (2020). International Outreach for university post-crisis. Quezon City, Philippines: QS Intelligence Unit.

Garcia, C. R., & Angeles, A. M. (2021). The Level of Utilization of DEPED Portal by Public Elementary School Teachers in Remote Areas of the Philippines. Asian Journal of Educational Research and Development, 9(2), 1-10.

Garcia, J. S., & Cortez, R. E. (2021). The Relationship between Utilization of DepEd Portal Video Lessons and Lesson Design: Basis for Teacher Efficacy. Journal of Education and Human Development, 10(2), 32-41.

Garcia, R., et al. (2022). The Relationship between DEPED Portal Utilization and Academic Performance among Elementary School Students in the Philippines. Journal of Education and Learning, 11(3), 25-38.

Ghanney, R. (2008). The Use of Instructional Materials in the Teaching and Learning of Environmental Studies in Primary Schools: A Case Study of Winneba. Retrieved from International Journal of Educational Research: https://www.ajol.info/index.php/ijer/article/view/41698

Gomez, R. M., & Acosta, M. T. (2021). The Relationship between Utilization of DepEd Portal Teaching Guides and Lesson Plans: Basis for Teacher Confidence. Journal of Education and Human Development, 10(3), 45-54.

Gonzales, A., et al. (2022). Utilization of DEPED Portal: A Case Study in the Philippines. Journal of Educational Technology Development and Exchange, 15(1), 25-38.

Lim, J., et al. (2022). Challenges Encountered by Teachers in Utilizing the DEPED Portal. Journal of Educational Technology Development and Exchange, 15(4), 20-35.

Llego, M.A. (2022) Towards a Sustainable and Working DepEd Commons Part II: A Framework. https://www.teacherph.com/deped-commons-framework/

LRMDS, D. o. (2018). Learning Resource Management and Development Manual. DepED LRMDS Portal.

Manalang, M. A., & Salcedo, N. M. (2021). Enhancing Teaching Strategies of Public Elementary School Teachers through the Use of the DepEd Portal. Journal of Educational Technology and e-Learning Research, 2(2), 56-64.

Mapunda, H. S. 2004. The use of internet by secondary school teachers: A case of twelve secondary schools. Dissertation for Award of MSc Degree at University of Dares Salaam, Tanzania

Martinez, J., et al. (2022). DEPED Portal Utilization and Academic Performance among Junior High School Students in the Philippines. Journal of Educational Technology Development and Exchange, 15(3), 32-45.

Natividad, J. C., & Sanchez, L. R. (2021). Enhancing the Planning Skills of Public Elementary School Teachers through the Use of the DepEd Portal Teaching Guides. Asian Journal of Education and Training, 7(2), 46-55.

Negros Oriental Learning Resource Portal (2021). http://negorlrmds.weebly.com/lrmds-vision--objectives.html

Pascual, M., et al. (2022). Guidelines to Support Parents in their Children's Utilization of the DEPED Portal. Journal of Education and Learning, 11(4), 12-25.

Ramos, E. D., & Flores, K. G. (2021). The Level of Utilization of DEPED Portal Video Lessons by Public Elementary School Teachers in Different Regions of the Philippines. Journal of Education and Practice, 12(13), 37-46.

Reyes, L. A., & Garcia, C. M. (2021). Enhancing the Teaching Practices of Public Elementary School Teachers through the Use of the DepEd Portal Video Lessons. Asian Journal of Education and Training, 7(1), 32-41.

Reyes, R., (2022). DEPED Portal Utilization Levels in Urban and Rural Schools in the Philippines. Journal of Education and Learning, 11(1), 45-58.

Reyes, M., et al. (2022). Challenges Encountered by Parents in Supporting their Children's Utilization of the DEPED Portal. Journal of Education and Practice, 13(4), 32-45.

Santos, L., et al. (2022). Differences in DEPED Portal Utilization between Male and Female Teachers in the Philippines. Journal of Education and Practice, 13(4), 32-45.

Santos, L., et al. (2022). Challenges Encountered by Students in Utilizing the DEPED Portal. Journal of Education and Learning, 11(4), 45-58.

Sipahi, E. (2020). Teacher resourcing TLMs practices and perceptions: Its effects on students' performance. Social Science Journal, 6, 119-128. https://purkh.com/index.php/tosocial/article/view/726

Susara, N. S. (2019, 10 June). Investigative Reports. Retrieved from Investigative Reporting Batch 2016: https://investigativereportingsite.wordpress.com/2016/05/13/the-potential-andproblems-of-lrmds/

Tan, K., et al. (2022). Student Engagement and Academic Performance in Grade 5 Learners. Journal of Education and Learning, 11(2), 65-78.

Tan, S., et al. (2022). The Effectiveness of a Teacher Training Program in Enhancing Teachers' Utilization of the DEPED Portal. Journal of Educational Technology Development and Exchange, 15(4), 45-58.

Torbila, C.J. (2021) Impact of Teacher Factor on the Utilization of LRMDS in the Division of Biliran. Impact Factor SJIF 2017:5.182 2018: 5.51, (ISI) 2020-2021: 1.361 E-ISSN: 2454-6615

Learning Resource Portal/Dashboard, Admin Panel, RO8 s. 2018

UNESCO (2020). COVID-19 Educational Disruption and Response Beirut, Lebanon.

UNESCO Learning Portal (2020). Brief 3: Learning and Teaching Materials Paris.

Villanueva, R. A., Dela Cruz, J. D., & Espiritu, E. S. (2021). The Relationship between Utilization of DepEd Portal and Student Learning Outcomes: Basis for Teacher Self-Efficacy. Journal of Education and Human Development, 10(2), 34-43.

APPENDIX A

FACULTY TRAINING FOR TEACHERS
IN-SERVICE TRAINING FOR TEACHERS (INSET)
June 14-16, 2023

I. **Project Title**: Technological Skills for 20th Century

II. **Project Proponent**: Silanganan Elementary School Faculty

III. **Implementing Agency:** Silanganan Elementary School, North II District, Division of Caloocan City

IV. **Project Rationale**:

The proposed Faculty Training Sessions on Utilization of DepEd Portal in School is a 3-days training seminar that will augment teachers' need of knowledge and skills towards proper way of utilizing the portal of the Department of Education for teaching-learning purposes. The said program will be conducted in Silanganan Elementary School, Division of Caloocan City using teachers as the beneficiaries of the said activity. The said seminar will be sponsored by the school on the aforementioned dates beginning June 14-16, 2023 with the use of MOOE or canteen fund.

June 14, 2023 will be scheduled for the topic about DepEd Portal: The overview about DepEd portal. It is also scheduled on Registration Process to DepEd Portal that will encourages teachers to use the portal in accessing their guide in teaching their respective subjects and students learning materials. June 15, 2023 will be scheduled for the Activity on harvesting students learning materials in the portal as well as the video clips that can be used in teaching-learning process in their respective subjects. June 16, 2023 will be scheduled for the awarding ceremony.

V. Objectives: Based on the Results-Based Performance Management System (RPMS) of the Department of Education made the above number of participants is expected to:

1. Familiarize teachers with the various features and tools of the DepEd Portal.
2. Provide hands-on training to teachers on how to use the DepEd Portal effectively.
3. Ensure that teachers are able to navigate the different sections of the DepEd Portal, such as the Learning Resource Management and Development System (LRMDS), the Learner Information System (LIS), and the Human Resource Information System (HRIS).
4. Train teachers on how to access and use the different types of educational resources available on the DepEd Portal, such as learning materials, lesson plans, and assessments.
5. Teach teachers how to create and manage their own accounts on the DepEd Portal, as well as how to access and use accounts for their students.

VI. Project Description: The three-day seminar will be conducted by the District Supervisors, Principal, Master Teachers, invited Resource Speakers and Selected Teachers and to be attended by all Teaching Staff of Silanganan Elementary School.

VII. Project Time Table: The training shall last for three (3) days and will start at 8:30 in the morning until 4:00 in the afternoon.

VIII. Personal Requirement: To have an organized and smooth flow of the seminar, different working committees are to be assigned:

TECHNOLOGICAL SKILLS FOR 2Oth CENTURY TEACHERS

Silanganan Elementary School

June 14, 15 and 16, 2023

Objective	Activities/ Strategies	Person Involve	Materials needed	Time Frame	Expected Outcome
Increase teachers' knowledge on the significance of the various features and tools of the DepEd Portal. Teach teachers how to manage their own accounts on the DepEd Portal.	Train teacher-beneficiaries to the following topics to enriched their knowledge about DepEd Portal/ LRMDS. ***Overview about DepEd Portal / LRMDS.** The Learning Resources Management and Development System (LRMDS) is designed to support increased distribution and access to learning, teaching and professional development resources at the Region, Division and School/Cluster levels of DepEd. ***The purpose of DepEd portal/LRMDS.** To develop, support and strengthen education management and learning support systems for improved access to quality basic education. ***The importance of LR/LRMDS.** The provision of adaptive learning resource systems, fully functioning at the region and division levels, effectively developing and distributing adequate and varied learning resources to teachers and learners from both the formal Basic Education and Alternate Learning systems. The LRMDS is designed to achieve the following objectives:	Resource Speaker, teacher - beneficiaries, seminar organizers	Ppt of the topics to be discussed, computer, projector, sound system, materials and equipment, and food for facilitators and participants	June 14, 2023	Increased teachers' knowledge on the DepEd Portal.

	1.Strengthened Learning Resource development and distribution systems at Regional and Divisional levels. 2.Improvement of instructional and learning materials system through support for the assessment, acquisition, adaptation, development, production and distribution of teaching/learning materials to schools. 3.Digitized available student learning materials (including from PASMEP, PROBE, PRODED, BEAM, TEEP, SEDIP, etc), particularly for reading in the early grades and TLE programs, English, Science and Mathematics in other grades, ADM and ALS. 4.Enhanced provisions of quality instructional and learning materials, particularly in reading in early grades and TLE, English, Science and Mathematics in other grades. 5.Modified and enhanced instructional and learning materials for implementing Alternative Delivery Modes and Learning Systems. 6.Improved development and utilization of Quality Assurance (including Monitoring and Evaluation) systems for provision and utilization of learning resources. 7.Development of ICT-enabled solutions in the three regions, integrated with national systems, to support the strengthening of the learning resource support systems. ***Where and how to access DepEd portal.** LR portal registration.				

	1.Go to: www.lrmds.deped.gov.ph 2.At the homepage, click Register. 3.Fill in the required information Important: access to learning resources vary depending on the email address used for registration. * DepEd email (ex. name.surname@deped.gov.ph) gives access to all learning resources available in the LR Portal - K to 12 Learners Materials and Teacher's Guides, ALS modules, Professional Development materials, and Media Gallery *Personal email/Non-DepEd email gives access to learning resources available except for K to 12 Teacher's Guides. ***How is Registration Process to DepEd Portal.** To create a new account, you must register to the LR Portal by doing the following steps: Go to Register page by clicking on the Register link on top of the main menu. Fill in all the required fields and click on the Register button. A message shall be sent to the e-mail address you have registered.				
Help teachers how to access and use the different types of educational resources available on the DepEd Portal, such	Workshop on Navigating, and downloading and uploading files on the DepEd portal. -In order for you to have complete access on the site, you need to register for an account. It is advisable to use your DepEd email to create your LR portal account.	Resource Speaker, teacher -beneficiaries, seminar organizers	Mobile phones/ Laptop/ Desktop Computers Computer, projector, sound system, venue	June 15, 2023 3	Well-equipped teachers and improvement on the Academic Performance of the learners.

as learning materials, lesson plans, and assessments.	-After doing the process, you can explore the site and download a resource. To access one, click Resources in the navigation bar. Click K to 12 Resources. -Choose any of the available resources. **Hands-on on the following;** -Harvesting students learning materials and video lessons in the portal. -Downloading of Teaching Resources from DepEd Portal. Evaluation / Presentation of Outputs		materials and equipment.		
To recognize attendees and resource speakers as well as the TWGs of the activity.	• Awarding of certificates to all the attendees and speakers.	Resource Speaker, teacher - beneficiaries, seminar organizers	Laptop/ projector, sound system, venue materials and equipment and certificates for the speakers and attendees.	June 15, 2023 3	

Working Committees

Officers of The Day	Attendance and Time Checker	Technical Assistance	Usher/Usherette/ Food Committee	Sound System
Kinder & Grade I				
Grade II & III				
Grade IV				
Grade V				
Grade VI				

IX. Monitoring and Evaluation

The DepEd Portal Utilization of Public Elementary Teachers and Academic Performance of Learners is a 3-day In-Service training Webinar with duration of 6 hours per day. It will be spearheaded by the researcher together with the SES Technical Working Group, which are consists of School LRMDS coordinator and ICT Teachers. They are responsible in implementing the program. Outputs of the activities will be submitted to the office of the School Head. After the completion

of program, a narrative report with documentation will be submitted to the school head's office. The DepEd Portal Utilization of Public Elementary Teachers and

Academic Performance of Learners training will be evaluated by the participants through a Quality Assurance and Measurement Evaluation Tool (QAME). The result of the evaluation tool will be used to address issues for the improvement of the program.

MONITORING AND EVALUATION TOOL

The proposed Faculty Training Sessions on Utilization of DepEd Portal in School Training Content and Design

Scale: 4 - Strongly Agree (SA) 3- Agree (A) 2 - Disagree(D) 1 - Strongly Disagree (SD).

	Program Objective, Content and Result	Strongly Agree	Agree	Disagree	Strongly Disagree
1.	Program objectives were fully achieved				
2.	Program content was sufficient to meet the objectives				
3.	The pacing and duration of the program were just right				
4.	This program is highly recommended to others				

I. Evaluation of Program

Overall benefit you gained from the program; suggested topics to be included in the future programs.

II. Evaluation of Technology

Administrative Arrangements	Strongly Agree	Agree	Disagree	Strongly Disagree
1. Program was well prepared and managed				
2. The registration process was organized and systematic				
3. Relevant information (web links, sessions, registrations, etc.) were available and accessible				
4. The members of the Technical Working Group (TWG) were efficient, responsible, and courteous in answering concerns via email/phone/text.				

	Best	Better	Bad	Worst
1. Quality of audio				
2. Interactivity				
3. Length of session				
4. Visual content and graphics				

What is your overall assessment of the training?

☐ Excellent

☐ Good

☐ Fair

☐ Poor

Do you have any comments, concerns, suggestions, or complaints about any aspect of the sessions? We are especially interested in feedback and suggestions that will help us improve future events.

III. Evaluation of Session and Facilitators

A. Speaker

	Strongly Agree	Agree	Disagree	Strongly Disagree
1. The Speaker was able to convey the expected learning.				
2. The speaker presented the subject matter in a clear and effective manner				
3. . The speaker encouraged participation				
4. The speaker answered questions clearly and completely				
5. The speaker managed the time effectively				
6. The speaker demonstrated a positive attitude				
7. The facilitator stimulated my interest in the subject matter.				
8. The facilitator's skills in the use of delivery support materials (the use of slide decks) aided my learning.				

B. On Topic/Session

	Strongly Agree	Agree	Disagree	Strongly Disagree
1. The learning objectives were clearly stated.				

2. The topics were well-organized and relevant.
3. The materials used in the session are clear and easy to understand.

Prepared by:

CRISTINA B. TAAY

THE AUTHOR

Cristina B. Taay is a Licensed Professional Teacher (LPT), a graduate of Bachelor of Elementary Education at St. Joseph's College, Borongan, Eastern Samar. She finished her Master of Arts in Education major in Educational Management at University of Caloocan City. She worked as Elementary Grade Teacher at St. Francis De Sales Academy, Inc. from school year 2005 to 2008. She served as officer of Faculty Association and AP Teachers' Club. She was designated as Grade Level Chairperson from June 2012 to March 2015. Moreover, she was also appointed as School ICT Coordinator from July 2019 up to present. On top of these, she is a proud MTAP Trainer from June 2012 to S.Y. 2015. She actively attended various School/District/Division trainings, seminars and workshops to continually improve her crafts professionally. Presently, she is a classroom teacher at Silanganan Elementary School. She is happily married to Mr. Reynold C. Taay and living with their four children namely Janela Cassandra, Gabriel Kristoffer, Jairos Kristan, and Rhinoa Katrina.

www.ingramcontent.com/pod-product-compliance
Lightning Source LLC
LaVergne TN
LVHW080457160826
845677LV00006B/1393